In Defense of Elitism

Also by William A. Henry III

The Great One

*Visions of America: How We Saw
the 1984 Election*

William A. Henry III

In

Defense

of

Elitism

DOUBLEDAY

New York · London · Toronto · Sydney · Auckland

PUBLISHED BY DOUBLEDAY
a division of Bantam Doubleday Dell Publishing Group, Inc.
1540 Broadway, New York, New York 10036

DOUBLEDAY and the portrayal of an anchor with a dolphin
are trademarks of Doubleday, a division of
Bantam Doubleday Dell Publishing Group, Inc.

Library of Congress Cataloging-in-Publication Data

Henry, William A., 1950–
In defense of elitism / William A. Henry III.—1st ed.
p.   cm.
1. Elite (Social sciences)—United States.
2. Equality—United States.   I. Title.
HN90.E4H45   1994
305.5′2′0973—dc20   94-11893
CIP

ISBN 0-385-46899-7

Printed in the United States of America
September 1994
First Edition

1   3   5   7   9   10   8   6   4   2

For the friends who egged me on, especially the handful willing to have me say so in public:

Jim Burrus
Kay Gardella
Tom Geyer
George Gowen
Diana Green
Kjell Hornslien

Acknowledgments

IN A SENSE this book, or for that matter any book, is the product of all the author's life experiences, which are too numerous and tedious to set down here, and of all the author's reading, the most salient of which is quoted in the text. So my thanks are more practically restricted to the people who contributed to the development of the ideas and rhetoric, either by their forbearance in listening or by the vigor of their rebuttal. Without distinguishing among them by degree of enthusiasm or horror for the ideas propounded, I'd like to thank Kent Allen, Margaret Barthelme, Eliot Berry, Alan Brinkley, Andrew Carron, Charlotte Chandler, Camille Chwalek, Kevin Conroy, Eric Copage, Lucille and Tony Davino, Nancy Dickerson, John Dorfman, Gwynneth Dunwoody, MP, Dan Dwyer, Steve Economides, Robert Elliott, Omar Figueroa, Reuven Frank, Craig Gilbert, Ramon Gonzalez, Jeff Guss, Phil Heathcote, Mimi Hirsh, Con Howe, Leon Jaroff, Marilyn Kengla, Paul LaCosta, Jr., Peter Lane, Al Lauber, Mark Mobley, Evangeline Morphos, Martin Mugar and the Art Institute of Boston, Pat, Tony, Paul and Neil Munn, Jon Nygaard, Billy O'Leary, Thomas Cruise Palmer, Tom Plate, Adam Redfield, John Robinson, Tom Sabulis, Sylvia Sandeen, Christine, Guido and Joseph Sandulli, Stephen Shanley, Janice Simpson, Doug Sivco, Margaret Garrard Warner, and Anne Cabot Wyman.

Professionally, this book and its author are indebted to my agent, Michael Carlisle of the William Morris Agency, and my editor, David Gernert, for their unquenchable enthusiasm and unfathomable patience. Personally, this volume owes whatever creative tension it has between traditionalist theory and liberal pragmatism to my late mother, Catherine Henry, who lovingly fought me tooth and nail on every idea herein. As always, the central support in my life is my wife, Gail, whose editing was irreplaceable and whose snorting skepticism surely saved me from even worse pomposity and bombast than survives in the succeeding pages.

My close friend and research assistant James Burrus helped collate and synopsize the boxes full of background materials I had accumulated. His robust humor and fine sense of the ridiculous are evident on every page that is even faintly amusing.

Contents

In Defense of Elitism

ONE

The Vital Lie

"Cooperation is in, competition is out."
—*The New York Times,* May 16, 1993

SOMEWHERE along Bill Clinton's path to the White House it dawned on me that the term "elitist," which I had matter-of-factly applied to myself and most of my fellow liberal Democratic friends for decades, has come to rival if not outstrip "racist" as the foremost catchall pejorative of our times. Once I began consciously looking, I found evidence everywhere—from tabloid newspapers to scholarly journals, from smirky game shows to sober academic discourse, above all in the public rhetoric of liberals and conservatives alike— that belief in any sort of elitism, and in the all-important hierarchy of values that must underlie such a belief, has been pushed outside the pale of polite discussion. The very word, used as a label, seems to be considered enough for today's rhetoricians to dismiss their opponents as defeated beyond redemption.

At first I was inclined to write off most of the invective as the familiar if unedifying business of the have-less many ganging up on the better-off few. Envy may be one of the seven deadly sins in theological circles, but it is a box office winner in every sort of ordinary conversation. Gradually and reluctantly, however, I realized that the wrath directed at elitism has less to do with money than with populist, egalitarian scorn for the very kinds of intellectual distinction-making I hold most dear: respect and even deference toward leadership and position; esteem for accomplishment, especially when achieved through long labor and rigorous education; reverence for heritage, particularly in history, philosophy, and culture; commitment to rationalism and scientific investigation; upholding of objective standards; most important, the willingness to assert unyieldingly that one idea, contribution or attainment is *better than* another. The worst aspect of what gets called "political correctness" these days is the erosion of the intellectual confidence needed to sort out, and rank, competing values. It used to be that intellectual debate centered on the results of such assessment. We have retrenched to the point that the very act of starting the process requires audacity—or, as opponents phrase it, insensitivity.

Not long before she died, anthropologist Margaret Mead speculated that the United States was entering a new Dark Ages of medieval mysticism and mumbo-jumbo, of belief based on self-interest, mob politics, and fear rather than research and open-minded inquiry. She was far more correct than even she dreaded. The great post–World War II American dialectic has been between elitism and egalitarianism. Both are deeply American, precisely because they are deeply European. They were arguably the chief competing tenets of the eighteenth-century Enlightenment that was in turn the wellspring of American identity. The tension between them has swung way out of balance, and the wrong side, the unthinking and nonjudgmental egalitarian side, has been winning. A brand of anti-intellectual populism is running amok, eerily reminiscent of the nineteenth-century Know-Nothing movement, albeit a mirror image of it in political terms. Where that movement centered on ugly nativism and exclusion, this one carries inclusion to its comparable extreme, celebrating every arriviste notion, irate minority group, self-assertive culture, and cockamamie opinion as having equal cerebral weight, and probably superior moral heft, to the reviled wisdom and attainments of tradition. This "multicultural" revisionism is sometimes refreshing and instructive, but more often merely silly and occasionally deeply harmful. Often accompanying it is the still more dangerous assumption that the only fair measure of any sifting mechanism is the demographic equality of results it produces, not the relationship between the results and attainments in the real world.

This phenomenon has been most conspicuously observed at universities, which are entrusted with the curatorship of our heritage but which have caved in almost entirely to the rigorous dogma of what might be termed "special pleading studies." These purportedly scholarly undertakings are really intended to redress historic grievances, sometimes by willfully misunderstanding and reinventing the past, as though altering the present and future were not reform enough. They also seek to instill, and then minister to, a paranoid sense of victimology among assorted self-proclaimed minorities. Examples of this cranky attitudinizing have been well publicized in the popular press, by this writer among many others, and will be discussed voluminously later in this screed. But one quick instance may help illuminate this discussion. The new Heath anthology of American literature, intended as the basis for the standard college survey course, pointedly begins with Native American Indian chants and Spanish voyager poetry rather than Pilgrim rhetoric, specifically to dispel the idea that the nation's root culture is northern European. Subsequent sections abound in writings by women and blacks; for example, there is more by Charlotte Perkins Gilman, a "rediscovered" writer popular among feminists, than by Hemingway. Wasps and Jews are systematically underrepresented. There is work by Updike but none by Cheever, a sampling from Bellow but not from Malamud, because one "needs" only a single example of the contemporary suburban Wasp or the urban Jew. All these writers are presumed, as a matter of course, to have merit almost wholly as anthropological artifacts rather than as artists. The notion of individual vision and expression—especially among artists of the ethnic or gender majority—is subordinated almost entirely to the idea of group identity.

Elementary and secondary schools, both public and private, are only a scintilla better. They are far less concerned with the

educational needs of the children they teach than with the
political yearnings of the adults who lobby them. The rewriting of curricula at every level is now frankly, unabashedly
described as a political process; ideas and even facts that are
deemed potentially offensive to any organized "victim" group
are brushed aside, for everyone must be guaranteed his (excuse
me, his-or-her or, perhaps, the odious antisyntactical evasion
"their") place at the table. The avowed purpose of many curricula, from Afrocentric studies in Baltimore public schools to
the gay studies minor at San Francisco State College, is to
encourage students to feel better about themselves, as though
there were no difference between the classroom and the counseling service. The emphasis is not on acquiring vocational
skills or sharpening one's reasoning. Indeed, in some circles—
and not just, alas, in California, from where such thinking
seems to emanate—rationality itself is argued to be a Western
cultural artifact, no more legitimate than other and more intuitive or primal ways of knowing the world. I have in fact
met quite a number of nominally educated, if doctrinaire,
people for whom the word "rational" is a withering insult, a
debate-stifling dismissal, apparently on a par with "elitist."

The academic rot (the "dead white European male" syndrome) is, alas, only the most flagrant manifestation of misguided egalitarianism. In the civil service and the private corporate world, affirmative action programs that were intended
to broaden the leadership population have been so misunderstood and misused (by cynical white male managers far more
than by minority applicants, it must be said) that their chief
effect has been, perversely, to de-credential those minority
achievers who rise entirely through diligence, industry, and
learning. I think of a Yale friend of mine who went on to
Harvard Law School and the Wharton School of Finance at
the University of Pennsylvania, then was on the partner track
at a big New York City law firm before leaving to take a big
job in New York State finance. For her first six months on the

job, she told me, it was obvious that every new person she met thought she had been hired because she was a black woman, and not because she had the best résumé in the room. Other black professionals to whom I told this story agree. Some continue to defend affirmative action—"Without it, we wouldn't be here at all," say a colleague of mine at *Time* and another close friend at *The New York Times*—but they all suspect it stigmatizes their accomplishments, even among fellow blacks.

In the mass media, a generation of elitist editors and writers who saw journalism, both print and broadcast, as a sacred opportunity to teach and uplift the citizenry has been supplanted by a mob of shameless panderers who "edit" by readership survey. They sample audience opinion and use that as the primary guide, so as to focus on topics that readers already know they want to hear about—as though no news were inherently more or less important than any other, only more or less popular, indeed as though readers already know what news is before they see it. This abandonment of the high ground is most conspicuous at the networks, and has been acknowledged to me (in my sometime capacity as media reporter) by such executives as Reuven Frank, then president of NBC News; Van Gordon Sauter, then president of CBS News (and now in the same role at the Fox network); and Av Westin, then principal deputy at ABC News. The new marketeering is also evident at newspapers, including *The New York Times,* with its proliferation of lifestyle and entertainment sections, and the ever more chatty *Washington Post,* to say nothing of *USA Today* and its countless local clones.

This rejection of pedagogy, this deliberate dumbing-down, is even more obtrusive in movies, television entertainments, and, especially, commercials, many of which congratulate the onlooker for ignorance coupled with blissful indifference. (Has there ever been a more boastfully anticerebral campaign than the ubiquitous beer company putdown of curiosity embodied in the slogan "Why ask why"? At least "Winston tastes good like a cigarette should" was merely ungrammatical, not aggressively dismissive of learning.)

In politics, where the business of surveying an audience and then groveling to it is naked—indeed, some supposedly respectable practitioners consider it the entire sum and substance of the enterprise—the degraded status of elitism was appallingly evident in the most recent presidential campaign. Witness the urgency with which both sides hastened to disassociate themselves from any whisper of the concept, let alone actual elite status, as though it were an anathema transcending ideology. In the most celebrated example, Vice President Quayle never quite clarified his attacks on a Hollywood "cultural elite," but he didn't have to. He needed only to evoke inchoate rage in the populace that anyone, whatever the level of intellectual or creative attainment to justify it, might consider himself *better than* anyone else. If Hollywood's self-labeled "creative community" were really so estranged from middle-American tastes and values, its products would not sell. Quayle's real goal was to avenge himself against entertainers who had mocked him with material drawn largely from his own documented malapropisms, and he obviously felt that "elitist" was the dirtiest mudball he could sling.

President Bush was, characteristically, a little subtler and blander in his attacks on Governor Clinton for having had enough brains and gumption to get to Oxford. This was vintage anti-elitism even if Bush did not speak the actual word. His import was twofold: that Clinton was too smart to be President, a notion that gets weirder and more disturbing the longer one looks at it; and that the electorate ought to vote based on envy and resentment toward their betters, an appalling onslaught made surreal by Bush's own status as a senator's son, prep-school smoothie, Phi Beta Kappa (how, one wonders?) at Yale, and (as was ostentatiously asserted) "self-made" oil millionaire—via a company he launched with money bor-

rowed from his rich uncle. In the wake of Bush's dethrone-
ment, such customarily thoughtful figures as Kevin Phillips,
the strategist who once forecast a permanent majority for his
Grand Old Party, warned that the party's future was gravely
imperiled. Its sin: despite Bush's and Quayle's denunciatory
rhetoric, a supposedly excessive attention to "elites."

On the left, the policies disparaging elitism were more sincere but the rhetoric was less snarly, perhaps because Clinton
and Al Gore were running as meritocrats who had burst to the
top on the basis of doing their homework. All around them,
however, oozed a miasma of disdain for hierarchies. Newly
elected Democratic Senator Patty Murray of Washington
praised her constituents for eschewing "elitists, wealthy legislators, or celebrities who never come home." Perhaps this was
just reflex populism, but it seemed to signal a depressing preference for being a Senator Pothole, preoccupied with constituent service and accessibility, over being a Senator Fulbright
type, sent off from some backwater to think great thoughts
and lead a nation. Barbara Jordan, the party's most eminent
woman, managed to link the twin opprobriums of our time in
a keynote speech at the party's national convention, where she
deplored "the thinly disguised racism and elitism of some
kinds of trickle-down economics." (I winced when she
equated elitism and racism, both because she should know
better—her public career has been the very embodiment of
Fulbrightian elitism—and also because if she could make this
easy verbal link, so could absolutely anyone.)

In my home state of New Jersey, all three candidates for the
1993 Republican nomination for governor—each a certifiable
conservative—berated one another as elitist throughout the
primary. In economic terms, they were asserting truth; each is
wealthy. The slurs were otherwise devoid of intellectual content. The vilification reached a high (or low) point of unin-
tentional comedy when the most right wing of the trio condemned targeted, policy-based tax cuts—specifically including

those designed to benefit the poor—as "elitist." In this through-the-looking-glass world, an egalitarian move was wickedly "elitist" while an elitist countermove would be laudably "egalitarian." However dimly lit the mind from which this utterance came, it was a dispiriting index of elitism's low esteem, even in reactionary circles.

Over in Europe, in whose culture many of the most controversial forms of elitism are alleged to be rooted, the present-day mea culpas are loud and frequent. Jacques Delors, the French socialist who as president of the European Community's executive branch came to personify the Common Market bureaucracy, apologized during 1992 for that institution as "too elitist and too technocratic." In the five hundredth anniversary year of Columbus's epic voyage, the Swedish Academy and its Norwegian counterpart gleefully corrupted the Nobel Prizes to join in the din of politically correct denunciation. The Peace Prize went to Guatemalan Indian leader Rigoberta Menchú, a woman, and the Literature Prize to Caribbean poet and playwright Derek Walcott, a black man. Both are worthy enough, but the reasons they were chosen are not. As was readily conceded, if not always for attribution, officials in Stockholm and Oslo wanted to avoid honoring anyone in the European humanities tradition during this particular year and instead sought to focus explicitly on people deemed victims of Columbus's colonial legacy. (Never mind that Menchú carried her political message via European-derived languages and technology, or that Walcott expressed himself and found a worldwide audience in the language of the ostensible oppressor. Forget that they and their countrymen escaped indigenous poverty and terror through such European-promoted notions as charity, economic opportunity, and individual freedoms and rights—not to mention modern medicine.) In 1993, eyebrows were raised when novelist Toni Morrison, a black woman, was chosen, less for embodying American culture than for challenging it. She is a writer adequate to the

Nobel's admittedly mixed past standards. One does wonder, however, to what extent pure literary merit won her the accolade.

While conceiving and writing this book, and simultaneously media watching (as press critic, among other callings, at *Time*), I happened upon only two even equivocally positive references to elitism in the course of nearly two years. Both were in conjunction with the self-consciously snooty realm of public television. (When I worked in Boston, station WGBH's call letters were said to stand for Well, God Bless Harvard, while a friend of mine who labored, rather more vigorously than his colleagues, at WNET in New York City referred to that institution's role as "Ivy League welfare.") Critic John O'Connor of *The New York Times* reviewed a twentieth-anniversary celebration of the *Great Performances* series by characterizing the producers and their efforts as "elite" or "elitist" six separate times in a single article, always with evident approval. The only daring thing was the approval; the description of the shows as "elitist" would have delighted many an antagonistic assistant professor inflamed with a political agenda. The other PBS citation was more ambiguous. A video production of Simon Gray's play *The Common Pursuit,* an off-Broadway and regional theater hit about the literary careers of several (admittedly live) white European males, featured a character saying "Someone's got to be elitist, especially at a time when no one else wants to be." I would have liked to shout out, from the safety of my couch, "Right on." But the speaker, the leading character, was portrayed as an arrogant, self-righteous prig and insufferable male chauvinist, which rather undercut his rallying cry.

By now, I can guess, some readers must think I fit the unappetizing sketch of that "elitist" stage-and-screen character rather more than I would ever admit. I can hear in my mind's ear the accusations of bigotry, the ideological pigeonholing, the myriad contumely customarily heaped upon those judged uncaring. And I suspect that before I am through, this book genuinely will offend all sorts of interest groups, organized or not. I know that merely telling friends I was writing a book with this title elicited loud giggles from those who were sure I must be joking, and gasps of horror from the rest. My wife said we ought to get an unlisted telephone. My mother, terminally ill when I agreed to write this volume, reacted with characteristic dark humor and ultraliberal fire: "Well, thank God I'll probably be dead before *that* gets published." I am fully aware that much of what I deplore as retrograde tribalism or wrongheaded moralism is regarded by large sectors of the population as progress. I am also painfully conscious that taking the postures I do may condemn me to accommodating some pretty strange bedfellows—racists, male supremacists, patriotic zealots, reactionaries, religious exotics, and assorted other creeps. I confess to being a white Ivy-educated male who is married and lives in the suburbs (in kind of a nice house, actually). Yet I am not a right-winger, and I hope I am not a nut. I am still a registered Democrat, a recipient of awards for civil rights writing from the National Conference of Christians and Jews, the Gay and Lesbian Alliance Against Defamation, and the Unity in Media contest based at historically black Lincoln University. I am a card-carrying member of the American Civil Liberties Union and a donor to abundant left-of-center social causes. My boyhood heroes were Hubert Humphrey and Martin Luther King, Jr. At a party in Washington some months ago I hurriedly crossed the room to avoid even being introduced to Pat Buchanan, and my wife and I have donated copiously to the electoral opponents of Jesse Helms.

This book really has a simple premise: that since modern America took shape at the end of World War II (a conflict that put women in the workplace, blacks in the front lines of combat, and veterans into college classrooms), nearly every great domestic policy debate has revolved around the poles of elitism and egalitarianism—and that egalitarianism has been winning far too thoroughly. This debate underlies the thorniest social issues of our era, from feminism, multiculturalism, and proposed bans on hate speech to affirmative action, racial quotas, the erosion of political parties, and the re-enshrinement of the more aggressive forms of "progressive" taxation. The same thinking is embedded, less overtly, in cultural changes—from the relentless debunking of heroes and heroism to the universal self-celebration of the masses via home Polaroids and camcorders, call-in radio shows and instant polls, Ross Perot's and other pols' video town meetings and even (oh mercifully waning fad!) karaoke machines. Talent, achievement, practice, and learning no longer command deference. Everybody is a star. Andy Warhol said everyone would have fifteen minutes of fame, and nonachievers by the millions have come to expect it as a birthright.

We have foolishly embraced the unexamined notions that everyone is pretty much alike (and, worse, should be), that self-fulfillment is more important than objective achievement, that the common man is always right, that he needs no interpreters or intermediaries to guide his thinking, that a good and just society should be far more concerned with succoring its losers than with honoring and encouraging its winners to achieve more and thereby benefit everyone. At times—indeed, at almost all times when educational policy is involved —we are as silly as the people in Garrison Keillor's fictional heartland, where *all* the children are claimed to be "above average." We have devoted our rhetoric and our resources to the concept of entitlement, the notion that citizens are not to ask what they can do for their country, but rather to demand what it can do for them. The list of what people are said to be "entitled" to has exploded exponentially as we have redefined our economy, in defiance of everyday reality, as a collective possession—a myth of communal splendor rather than simultaneous individual achievements.

Save perhaps in the statistics-dominated realms of sports and finance, where accomplishment remains readily quantifiable and seemingly ideologically neutral, American society has lost the confidence and common ground to believe in standards and hierarchies. We have taken the legal notion that all men are created equal to its illogical extreme, seeking not just equality of justice in the courts but equality of outcomes in almost every field of endeavor. Indeed, we have become so wedded to this expectation that our courts may now accept inequality of outcomes as prima facie proof of willful bias. We have distorted public rhetoric to the point that no one may say what everyone knows, that the emperor has no clothes— that is, that the people offered up as the result of meritocratic searches are often the beneficiaries of quotas, political mandates, and unacknowledged double standards. When the reprehensible James Watt was sacked as President Reagan's interior secretary, he was not being punished for pillaging public lands to benefit private commercial interests, nor for despoiling the wilderness, nor for permitting the Environmental Protection Agency to devolve into a criminal organization, although he could have been charged with all these failings. He was ousted for daring to say of a panel he had recruited, "We've got a black, a woman, two Jews, and a cripple—and we've got quality." He had violated the unwritten code, which is that such people are to be sought on the basis of quotas, then presented as the yield of a purely talent-based search. The official pretense is that in a truly unbiased world, a talent-based search would lead to exactly this sort of mix. There is, of course, no hard evidence that this would be true in a perfect world, and it would surely be false at some times and in some circumstances. Given the unproportional distribution of education and job experience in the United States, it may be false far more often than true of the world we actually live in. But saying so, as Watt learned, is the one unforgivable sin.

In the pursuit of egalitarianism, an ideal wrenched far beyond what the founding fathers took it to mean, we have willfully blinded ourselves to home truths those solons well understood, not least the simple fact that some people are better than others—smarter, harder working, more learned, more productive, harder to replace. Some ideas are better than others, some values more enduring, some works of art more universal. Some cultures, though we dare not say it, are more accomplished than others and therefore more worthy of study. Every corner of the human race may have something to contribute. That does not mean that all contributions are equal. We may find romantic appeal, esthetic power, and even political insight in cultures that never achieved modern technological sophistication. That does not mean we should equate them with our own. It is scarcely the same thing to put a man on the moon as to put a bone in your nose. And even were all cultures equal, that would not mean they made equal contributions in the specific shaping of the American ideal. In the effort to wish it so, we have warpingly redefined contribution and reduced its meaning. It is not necessarily a conspiracy of silence that the historical record is so thin in detailing women painters and writers of the early Renaissance or black nuclear physicists and Hispanic political leaders of the early twentieth century. Sometimes the record is thin because the accomplishments were too. I expect many people will reflexively find these observations racist. But I am not asserting that, say, people of African descent cannot compete equally—only that their ancestral culture did not give them the tools and opportunity to do so. To me the real racism lies in the condescending assumption that we must equate all cultures to assuage African Americans, or any other minorities, instead of challenging them to compete with, and equal, the best in the culture where they live now.

Many groups have been held down by past circumstances but should now be able to contribute equally. A healthy society must be prepared to embrace all people of talent. Yet in order to motivate and reassure them for the future, we cannot reinvent the past to pretend that the dispossessed made glorious contributions then, or that studying the quotidian existence of bygone peasants and serving wenches will more than marginally enlighten us about the past's richest legacy, the high-culture attainments for which these serfs provided, at best, support staff.

Perhaps the foregoing rhetoric seems not so much objectionable as excessive, the pursuit of a gnat with an elephant gun. You may have managed to overlook the incident, discussed in detail in a later chapter, by which a mute girl won in federal court the right to enter a speech contest on the basis that it was elitist to exclude her from a competition for which she plainly lacked the vital qualification. You may have been spared the Associated Press report about a government commission assigned to research the so-called glass ceiling that ostensibly keeps women and minorities from rising beyond the midlevel of executive hierarchies. A Bush appointee to that commission, hence a presumed conservative or at least moderate, said she was determined to defer indefinitely the question of where and indeed whether such a ceiling actually exists, because she did not want to waste time on anything impeding the vastly more important task of accumulating "stories"—which is to say, unchecked anecdotal claims that bias rather than material insufficiency or character flaw has constrained particular people's ambitions. Anyone who has ever spent even a week involved in personnel matters knows that there is hardly an employee alive who sees his sidetracking as resulting from his own weaknesses. In these people's minds, it's always and automatically prejudice that debars them. Only sometimes are they right.

You may also have missed the round of critical applause for Edward W. Said's explanation that the true import of the works of Jane Austen and other classic novelists is that they validated imperialism and that the most meaningful judgment to levy against them and their past admirers is that they failed to "advocate giving up colonialism," as though political correctness were not only the measure but the meaning of literature. In addition, you may have overlooked the renaming of the Custer National Battlefield. By act of Congress, it is to be known henceforward as the Little Bighorn National Monument. The change was made in deference to American Indians (I decline to call them Native Americans until someone effectively debunks the theory that they, too, are immigrants —from Siberia a long time ago. As far as I can tell, about the only Native Americans are dinosaurs and skunks). Tribal leaders objected to a name that commemorated a uniformed United States general officer who died honorably in combat pursuing the stated objectives of his government. Instead, the Indians argued, the battlefield name should commemorate their victory and the ensuing slaughter of every white U.S. soldier the Indians could find. The president of a local college said, as part of the ceremony, "Two victories have been won here, one hundred sixteen years apart"—leaving no doubt that the loser on each occasion was the white race. An elder of the Northern Cheyenne, Austin Two Moons, added, "Now we have to try to forget what happened a hundred years ago." What happened, of course, is that a technologically superior civilization defeated an inferior one, setbacks such as Little Bighorn notwithstanding. But victory and conquest are too elitist to be cheered.

If you accept with me that there has been a discernible, maybe even deplorable, change in national values, you may nonetheless wonder whether elitism is automatically good and egalitarianism invariably evil, or vice versa, and you may be perplexed in any case as to what democracy means if not equality. Definitions are irksome, consisting as they tend to of ten percent axiom and ninety percent hedging and exceptions. Ideally I would prefer to respond the way Supreme Court Justice Potter Stewart reacted to obscenity, saying he might not be able to describe it abstractly but would recognize it when he saw it. I can scarcely hope, however, to sustain this argument much further, let alone at book length, without submitting to specificity.

It is customary in writing of this sort to proceed from dictionary definitions, although they rarely engage satisfactorily the complexities of what a word implies in everyday commerce. The battered Random House edition that serves my household characterizes egalitarianism as a philosophy "asserting, resulting from or characterized by belief in the equality of all men" and assesses elitism as "practice of or belief in rule by an elite" or, secondarily, "consciousness of or pride in belonging to a selected or favored group." These definitions are all right as far as they go but, perhaps because the dictionary is a quarter century old, they don't go very far.

Egalitarians—or at least the sort who rile me—believe that all humans are equal ("men" being no longer a politically correct synonym for mankind) and, worse, that they *should be,* on a more or less permanent basis, whatever the real-world differences in their performance and contribution. However much Karl Marx may have been rejected by the nations that once enshrined him and ostensibly followed his dicta, American egalitarians continue to believe Marxian romantic twaddle about the invariable blamelessness of the unaccomplished. They argue that talent is distributed absolutely evenly along class and educational lines, in defiance of everything we know about eugenics. Consequently, they insist that differences in attainment are explained entirely by social injustice. Egalitarians fear and detest the competitive impulse. They regard exploration, conquest, and colonization as having been unrelievedly barbaric and destructive, thereby mulishly overlooking the impact those movements had in dispersing administratively and technologically superior cultures and compelling inferior ones to adapt. Egalitarians are the sort who are trying to end ability tracking in elementary and sometimes secondary education, on the theory that bright children ought to be helping slow ones rather than maximizing their own achievements and pulling ahead. (I'm not making this up. This is actually popular, if not prevailing, educational theory.) Not far below the surface, this attitude embodies a Marxian belief that the smart pupils' intelligence is not theirs alone to allocate and command but is instead a communal asset to be deployed for the whole class's good.

The same impulse is spreading into athletics, which used to be a safe haven for striving. *The New York Times* reported in a May 1993 front-page article that if games are to be played, increasingly an elementary school class is apt to be divided into so many teams that no one is the last chosen. Children are thus supposedly shielded from noticing who is better or worse. For the most part, games and scores are avoided altogether in favor of self-development. Running is not necessarily timed; basketball hoops are adjusted in height and distance to fit each pupil's capacity. The point is not to measure oneself against absolute standards but to feel good about exercise and taking part. That is about as concise and benign an embodiment of egalitarianism as I can imagine. And I still think it is pernicious.

Elitists of equal misguidedness, and some of outright menace, permeate American society. I hold no brief for those who consider themselves superior by virtue of birth or theology—those who believe in the natural dominance of men or white people or Christians or heterosexuals (or of women or blacks or Muslims or homosexuals). To belong proudly to a selected or favored group is morally repellent when something other than learning and achievement serves as the basis for that selection or favoritism. (In my mind, this applies to exclusive country and city clubs, however private they claim to be, and I consider it a valid claim to raise against appointees to public office.) Belief in rule by an elite is no better than bigotry when ability is not the sole basis for admission to the circle of the elect.

The kind of elitists I admire are those who ruthlessly seek out and encourage intelligence and who believe that competition—and, inevitably, some measure of failure—will do more for character than coddling ever can. My kind of elitist does not grade on a curve and is willing to flunk the whole class. My kind of elitist detests the policy of social promotion that has rendered a high school diploma meaningless and a college degree nearly so. (All right, a Harvard degree means something. But what is the value of "honors" when up to two thirds of Harvard undergraduates have been getting them?) My kind of elitist hates tenure, seniority, and the whole union ethos that contends that workers are interchangeable and their performances essentially equivalent. My kind of elitist believed that maybe the worst thing about Japanese business was the de facto lifetime job guarantee it offered, and saluted the recent erosion of that pledge.

Egalitarianism has done great good for American society. Who can dispute the rightness of ensuring legal counsel for indigent defendants in criminal cases or of compelling employers to fork over the pensions they promised to faithful and productive workers? Without the egalitarian impulse to ensure the funding of public schools in poor areas as well as rich ones, we could have no meaningful elitist impulse in judging those schools' graduates.

Wait a minute, I can hear ideological opponents expostulating, it can never be as easy to learn in a poverty neighborhood's school as in a plush one's. Fairness does not compel giving way to egalitarianism to that extreme. Opportunity does not need to be exactly equal. It needs only to exist. For the talented and motivated, that will be enough. The rest may have a harder time. So be it. The vital thing is not to maximize everyone's performance, but to ensure maximal performance from the most talented, the ones who can make a difference. Society typically makes the opposite and erroneous call; it underemphasizes winners and overassists mediocrities. That egalitarian style makes society more manageable politically, but at the price of productivity, and it ought to change.

What of democracy, then? It is unquestionably modern America's greatest gift to the rest of the world, at once the end toward which oppressed nations strive and the best means to get there. Economic freedom and intellectual creativity thrive most richly in a democratic environment. And democracy, in its purest form, unquestionably epitomizes the notion of egalitarianism. The scholar's vote counts no more or less than the slacker's. The decision-making that results is often dispiriting to an actual majority of the electorate; every presidential election year, large numbers of voters describe their "favorite" as simply the best of a bad lot. As Churchill dryly observed, democracy is the worst form of government, except for all the others. The irresistible impulse throughout American history has been toward broader participation, extending the vote to blacks, to women, to people who cannot read and write, to people who cannot even communicate in English, the national language. Universal voting is so unquestioned a public good that in 1993 Congress enacted the long-debated "motor voter" bill to register people when they acquire driver's licenses, on the theory that anyone's participation, even if ignorant and fleetingly motivated, enriches the collective judgment.

Can democracy be reconciled with elitism? The answer is that in our society, it already has been. America is not a democracy pure and simple. Ours is a democratic *republic* in which certain fundamental rights—private property, freedom of unpopular speech, religious eccentricity, and legal precedent, to name just a few—are permanently sequestered from assault by violent, ephemeral expressions of popular will. This is, moreover, a *representative* democracy, and the representatives chosen are by and large *un*representative of the norm by virtue of superior talent, intellect, and drive. That expectation is implicit in the aphorism "May the best man win." Voters repeatedly reject insurrectionist candidates who parallel their own ordinariness, even candidates who vow to further the individual voter's interests, in favor of candidates of proven character and competence. This persistent if unarticulated elitism is compelling evidence for differentiating between egalitarianism and democracy.

The same mechanism works even more overtly in the selection of judges. Cronyism is rarely tolerated by the public. Intellectual distinction is considered the prime requisite, valued above ideology and certainly far above compatibility with the common man. The same is true of senior cabinet posts. It is not true, to be sure, of ambassadorships, where relative nobodies with deep pockets are so usual as to be clichés. That is probably because these posts are customarily sinecures, of trivial importance in the shaping of policy.

Once in situ, all high office holders are expected to conduct themselves in elitist fashion. They may make faint nods to egalitarianism by giving up the chauffeured limousine. When it comes to policy, however, they are urged to trust their brains and chart their own courses. Officials who depart from the majority will of their constituencies are less apt to be branded as traitors than to be applauded as profiles in courage. Egalitarianism reasserts itself only in the biennial or quadrennial rituals by which these office holders, or the leaders who appointed them, resubmit themselves to the popular will. While Ross Perot has dangerously proposed to upset this equation by the use of town meetings, telephone polls, and similar plebiscites playing to cranks and hysterics, that bad idea is going nowhere—not least because much of the electorate when polled for its opinions of the biggest issues will respond that it doesn't know enough to have an informed opinion. Translation: Let the elite do it.

If federal government implicitly embodies elitism, government at the state level is, by contrast, responsible for the most destructive egalitarian maneuver of my lifetime—the proliferation of lotteries. Politicians see these games as easy means of raising revenue. Educators are co-opted because school aid is typically a primary beneficiary. Virtually the only serious objections come from do-gooders who worry that the poor are being induced to risk money they can ill afford. Even that argument is offset by the claim of other do-gooders that what the downtrodden are buying is that irreplaceable commodity, hope.

What gets overlooked is the disturbing unstated message to the masses, win or lose: that their chance of success depends on the whims of fate rather than on their own hard work and talent. Worse, the lottery mentality often translates into an assumption that all life is a game of chance, all success accidental, the wealthy and powerful simply lucky rather than accomplished. When daydreams substitute for plans, when wishing seems more appropriate than work, when envy gains yet another rationale, the whole society is the loser.

The lottery mentality extends far beyond the off-track-betting windows and the grocery store queues for pick-six tickets. The airwaves are awash, especially in daytime when the unemployed and indigent are a larger percentage of the audience, with commercials soliciting cases for cheapjack personal injury lawyers. These hucksters promise big canasta to everyone who has sustained (or imagined) the slightest mishap. Yes, we are in every regard a litigious society. But we are also a nation still in the grip of the Gold Rush and much of our litigation is an expression of the belief that the only way to get rich is quick. Friends who have sat as jurors in personal injury cases have described to me the efforts of their fellows—especially the unemployed, housewives, and others without secure personally earned income—to vote lottery-size verdicts for piddling events. One recalls hearing a nonworking wife say, "We could change this person's whole life." That was the speaker's rationale for urging a two-million-dollar award to someone who lost a single joint of the little finger on the hand he doesn't even write with. What troubles me is not just the cost or the moral corruption implicit in such cases, but the further erosion of personal responsibility in favor of the idea that life is luck.

Arguing for elitism may appear to fly in the face of the most nearly universal American ideal, the belief in upward mobility. In theory, there is nothing to prevent someone of whatever social class from absorbing a traditional education and using his reasoning skills to economic and social advantage. In practice, however, anything that strengthens the intellectual status quo tends to enhance the career prospects of those born to privilege, if only because they are more apt to grasp both how to get such an education and why they should bother. Social critics who are more concerned with the demographics of outcomes than with the integrity of the process have been drawn to assorted egalitarian or, more precisely, anti-elitist schemes and dogmas as a means of nullifying such built-in advantages and leveling the playing field. The normally estimable Mickey Kaus, in his *The End of Equality*, proffers just such well-meaning fiddle-faddle. After waxing moony over the desirability of such ephemeral societies as revolutionary Catalonia during the Spanish Civil War, about which he admiringly quotes Orwell that this was a place where "waiters and shop-workers looked you in the face and treated you as an equal," he worries that contemporary America is becoming *too meritocratic!* He acknowledges that much of intelligence is hereditary, that class differences play only a secondary role in allocating places on the career and economic ladder, yet still he worries about "the loser problem." It is bad for society, he says, and morally troublesome to boot, that some people will end up less equal than others. He perceives, in the cosmic whim by which some are born smart and beautiful and others dim and plain, a "fairness problem"—ipso facto a problem beyond the capacity of any society to solve. Here is Kaus at his most worrying: "The more the economy's implicit judgments are seen as being fair and based on true 'merit' (and 'equal opportunity'), the more the losers will tend to feel they deserve to lose, the easier it will be to equate economic success with individual wealth, and the greater the threat to social equality." It is hard to read that and not feel one has ventured into Cloud-Cuckooland. What he's saying is this: Losers who lose on the basis of merit should be shielded from thinking their losing is merited; winners who win fairly should be barred from feeling comfort and pride. For Kaus's generation (which is also my own and, not coincidentally, the generation that has promoted egalitarianism across the social fabric), much of the image of an ideal social equality, all classes tumbled together cheek by jowl, derives from one's days as a college student. The baby boom took its college experience very, very seriously, not least because the rest of the country did too—fascinated then, as at each stage of our existence, by our sheer numbers. The warm and fuzzy memories of adolescent insights into the virtues of social equality tend to exclude two vital facts about the fleeting nature of those perceptions.

The first of these facts is that boomers remember being more or less equal with everyone else in college because, for the last time in their lives, they *were* more or less equal. None of them was doing anything useful or constructive in economic terms. They were, with minor exceptions, all and equally a drain on the national purse. To be sure, they provided employment for their teachers and the rest of the university apparat. To be sure, some of them had part-time or even full-time jobs (although the vast majority were working simply to support the university bureaucracy, a self-sustaining nonindustry). But in terms of the kind of creative or entrepreneurial endeavor that breeds national wealth, and with it social and economic hierarchies, as students the baby boomer collegians were by definition out of the running. This equality of uselessness would, however, evanesce as soon as they ceased to be students and accepted employments of, inevitably, varying worth. The memory of equality would continue to permeate their nostalgic recollections of youth in the same vivid but misleading way that rationing coupons or the universal draft permeated the maunderings of their parents' generation.

The second vital fact, which derives from the first, is that there was something utterly bogus about the idea of the worker-student alliances so widely celebrated, in rhetoric at least, by radical collegians of the era. The students, like the workers, lived on tight budgets and modest incomes; indeed, they often competed for the same housing. The students, like the workers, were closely supervised and constantly evaluated and felt essentially powerless toward their overlords. But this status was temporary for the students and permanent for the workers. The laboring classes generally felt that they weren't going anywhere—that their future would be pretty much like their present but with more gray hair. The students knew they would move on to bigger and better. Indeed, the dirty little secret of sixties radicalism—I know, I was there—was that many of its most aggressive proponents were those who felt the deepest elitist yearnings. Their avarice was transmuted into leftist rage by the fear that they might not prevail, that in a fiercely meritocratic contest they might not qualify for the house with the white picket fence and the Beamer in the three-car garage. To them, society was unjust if it would not give them what they wanted. Their very definition of fairness, while shouted to the skies in egalitarian terms, was the result of thwarted or imperiled elitist ambition. This is the "loser problem" Kaus talks about; it is not a pretty sight. It brings to mind a joke that Ronald Reagan loved to tell about Russia, one that several Russian friends of mine have confirmed as epitomizing the national character during the Leninist egalitarian idyll. Three recently dead men are brought before the throne of God and told they may each have one wish. The Briton asks for an end to war. The American asks for an end to hunger. The Russian smiles slyly and says, "In my village, I have a neighbor who has a cow. I do not have a cow. I wish that my neighbor's cow shall sicken and die."

The point of elitism is not, when all is said and done, to promote envy or to enlarge the numbers of society's losers. It is to provide sufficient rewards for winning, and sufficient support for ideas that have shaped past progress and that might aid future progress so that society as a whole wins—that is, gets richer, better educated, more productive, and healthier. There is plenty of room for upward mobility in such a system. Indeed, the idea of general progress more or less demands it. If the entire social order were to rise in concert, with no one ever breaking free of his place, there would be very little incentive for movement at all. Instead, the history of America is by and large a history of upward mobility, for successive ethnic groups as a whole and for their ablest members in particular. The impetus for overthrowing a system that worked so well, providing an all but universally acknowledged social justice, comes notably from four groups that present sui generis problems that the old order seems unready to solve.

The first problem is of integrating homosexuals, whose success and contributions are undeniable but whose past attainments have come at the price of denial of their basic identity, a price many of them are no longer willing to pay. To many homosexuals, the old elitism and cultural heritage are inextricably entwined with a religious value system that declared their lives immoral and a more recent psychological value system that, until a few years ago, declared their love deranged.

Closely related is the problem of women, who see any celebration of the past as an enshrinement of a social construct in which they were unneeded for much beyond procreation and support services. To appreciate the past is, in their view, to strengthen the argument that the world got along just fine before feminism and therefore need not swiftly change. With both homosexuals and women, the problem is that they are categorically different from ethnic groups both in their own minds and in those of onlookers, and thus their accession to power might not be entirely assured in traditional elitist models of upward mobility. Their rise would not just require others to make room, it would require that those already in place redefine their own bases for judging self-worth.

The third problem category is Hispanics, who are by now almost certainly the largest minority group in the United States (albeit not all of them legally here). They are pretty close to being a traditional ethnic group, although Hispanic activists are at pains to point out that Hispanics may be of any race and come from a wide variety of national origins. The difficulty with Hispanics is that they want to change the rules for upward mobility. They claim, by right of sheer numbers, the power to rise without accepting the shared national language, English, or entering fully into a common American culture. This demand is viewed by the longer-established ethnic groups, especially blacks, as a bid for special privileges— and they are right. It is.

The most nettlesome problem of all is posed by the black community (something of a misnomer, inasmuch as many middle-class blacks take great efforts to distance themselves, especially residentially, from their underclass racial kin). Blacks have been upwardly mobile, especially since the civil rights movement. But they are not mobile enough to suit them or to quell the consciences of much of the white majority. Racism has certainly played a major past role in hampering their rise. For the most part, blacks remain visually identifiable at a glance, furthering the possibility that racism still holds sway. Yet there is a growing recognition that something else besides racism may be holding blacks back. The fundamental division between what are loosely called "black conservatives" (a catchall used to embrace everyone from true right-wingers like Thomas Sowell and Walter Williams to such look-again liberals as Shelby Steele and Yale law professor Steve Carter, author of *Reflections of an Affirmative Action Baby)* is that the "conservatives" suggest that blacks may be to some degree responsible for their problems, while the mainstream black community takes the posture that every disadvantage is, ultimately, whitey's fault. Only a handful of white thinkers are willing to stand up to this victimology. Reviewing *American Apartheid,* a book that posits residential segregation as the primary cause of a black underclass, welfare scholar Charles Murray debunks the chronologies underlying the thesis. Then he notes that there are some valid reasons beyond stereotyping for why whites keep neighborhoods segregated. "The problem is that many of these 'negative stereotypes,'" he adds with deadly understatement, "are founded on empirically accurate understandings about contemporary black behavior compared to contemporary white behavior." The prose is a model of scholarly euphemism; the content is a slap in the face to romantics who believe that treating all people as equals will instantly make them so. Even Jesse Jackson has underscored the importance of holding individuals responsible for their antisocial behavior, most notably in his much-quoted chagrin at looking back behind him and being relieved to note that the young men following him were white.

Each of these problem groups—by which I mean that their cases pose analytic problems, not that there is a problem in the mere fact of their existence—will be discussed in subsequent chapters. So will public schools, colleges, unions, the economic system, popular culture, mass media, politics, and such ticklish topics as the retarded and the handicapped (the real world's nomenclature, if not necessarily theirs). Plus, of course, the intellectual mulligan stew that seethes in the pot labeled multiculturalism.

But it would be folly to focus on these specifics without some words on the general subject of "superior" and "inferior" cultures—a concept that is bound to raise as much Cain as anything in this book and a basis for most of the discussion in the chapters to come. A superior culture, as I see it, is one that fulfills all or most of seven basic criteria.

First and foremost, a superior culture preserves the liberty of its citizens. A society may be disadvantaged in this quest by reasons of geography, economics, size relative to its neighbors, and so on. But in essence, a culture that maintains autonomy is superior. One that fails to fend off invaders, or that permits large numbers of its inhabitants to be taken into slavery, is on its face inferior. Whatever moral or spiritual or other virtues a conquered culture may offer, they cannot redeem the loss of freedom.

Second, a superior culture provides a comfortable life, relatively free from want, for the plupart of its citizens. It would be foolish to draw a straight line equation on this principle. The accident of oil wealth should not by itself make Kuwait rank as superior to, say, Italy, or even India. But in general a valid culture will lift its people above a subsistence economy and afford the merits of trade and entrepreneurship.

Third, a superior culture promotes modern science, medicine, and hygiene and otherwise maximizes the health, comfort, and longevity of its citizens. By medicine I mean Western medicine, pending persuasive nonanecdotal research into the merits of any other kind. By science I emphatically do not mean numerology, mysticism, astrology, ESP, or any of the new age crapola that beguiles second-rate minds (and that is normally, and correctly, identified as foreign to mainstream Western culture). By hygiene I mean not only the use of toilets and the preservation of potable drinking water but a rational acceptance of birth control and an attitude neither phobic nor reckless toward sex.

Fourth, a superior culture produces permanent artifacts that express esthetic and humanistic principles appreciated by other cultures. In general, the bigger and more numerous these artifacts are, and the more sophisticated and varied the craftsmanship they manifest, the better. Hence Chartres Cathedral is superior to any tribal mask or religious totem, not because it is European or Christian, but because it evidences greater human ingenuity and invention. The permanence of such artifacts is admittedly a matter of chance. Sheer antiquity diminishes the number and quality of cultural remnants. Much of the Parthenon's sculpture is eroded or outright gone, and most of Greek drama is lost, although in both cases what survives is breathtaking. Similarly, the cultures that wind up as conservators of a region's patrimony are often inferior enough that they fail to protect their heritage (along with, more often than not, the liberty of their citizens). One can hardly blame classical Indian culture, for example, for the disgraceful way that vast carpets, exquisite little Mogul miniature paintings, and gossamer-grand palaces are left to rot unprotected in humid and polluted modern air in, for example, the once-regal city of Jaipur. But by and large, the greater the culture, the more of a legacy it leaves, so that even the ravages of time cannot erase its memory.

Fifth, a superior culture provides widespread, rigorous general education and ensures an essentially meritocratic admissions system, so that the chief talents of each generation will be fully exploited. A culture that leaves its people in agrarian ignorance, or that educates only a priestly or partisan elite, must be judged inferior, whether it exhibits the moral dignity of Tibet or the moral squalor of Libya.

Sixth, a superior culture expands, by trade or cultural imperialism or conquest or all of the above, and will find its tenets embraced by the erstwhile captives even when the era of expansion is over. Think of the Mongols in China (though scarcely a trace remains of them in the West), the Moors in Iberia, the Spanish in South America.

Seventh, a superior culture organizes itself hierarchically, tends toward central authority, and overcomes tribal and regional divisions, all without suppressing the individual opportunity for self-expression and advancement. A culture that allows an individual the opportunity to paint on a larger canvas, as it were, is patently superior to one that compels him to think no further than his clan or valley.

I am tempted to add an eighth criterion, that a superior culture is not theocratic. But that would overvalue my personal taste and beliefs. While religious domination of a society is plainly backward and maladaptive in the modern world—for one thing, it more or less compels a society to focus inward rather than expand—some if not most of the greatest cultures of the past were inflexibly theocratic at least in theory. (One suspects that then, as now, sovereignty in practice was a touch more pragmatic.)

I expect these definitions to provoke much dispute. That is because, like everything else connected with elitism, they produce some politically inconvenient outcomes. I envision people reading along contentedly enough through each of the criteria until they realize, with abrupt horror, exactly whose oxen are being gored. Such resistance only reinforces the central point of this volume. In the unspoken assumptions that underlie everyday discourse, we are an elitist society because nothing else is logical. In the exchange of lies and euphemisms that constitutes the surface of polite discourse, we are egalitarian, because nothing else is diplomatic.

Ibsen, in *The Wild Duck,* says that every human being survives because of some vital lie. So, perhaps, does every nation. Our vital lie is egalitarianism. Paul Fussell, in his astute and snarly book *Class,* quotes Roger Price as saying, "Democracy demands that all of its citizens begin the race even. Egalitarians insist that they all *finish* even." In our honest moments we know that they cannot so much as start even. There are differences from birth, not only of class and privilege, but of brains and drive—qualities that can only be enhanced, not instilled, from the outside. Still, we persist in demanding that everyone finish even. We define it as injustice when they don't. As the novelist Robert Stone observed on the op-ed page of *The New York Times* in March 1993: "In our radical interpretation of democracy, our rejection of elites, our well-nigh demagogic respect for the opinions of the unlearned, we are alone." The defense of elitism that our society so sorely needs is ultimately nothing more than the defense of common sense.

TWO

"Good Old Golden Rule Days"

"From condom distribution to addiction counseling, schools are spending more and more time dealing with social problems rather than basic education."
—*The Wall Street Journal,* May 27, 1993

IN A COMBINED second- and third-grade class conducted in rural Johnson City, New York, in the spring of
1993, pupils who were engaged in a study of the concept of
perimeters tried to find a way to involve a classmate who is
mentally retarded and unable to speak. Their solution: to turn
her into a giant ruler. They coaxed her to lie on a pad and
used her to do their measuring. This incident, reported in *The
New York Times,* was neither a scandal nor, alas, an anomaly.
In many school districts these days, ordinary classrooms are
encumbered with formerly sequestered "special education"
students who are ill equipped to learn and who impede the
progress of those who can. The same quixotic liberalism that
led to the "deinstitutionalization" of genuine lunatics, who
now stand on street corners swaying and talking to themselves,
has taken hold of public education. Egalitarians have pro-
claimed that the self-esteem and limited learning opportunities of the disabled are more important than the advancement
of the fit, let alone the gifted. Parents of the mentally handicapped, wishing to sustain the illusion that their children are
normal, and educators committed to tolerance more than to
education have joined forces to compel schools to integrate
even the most different children into the ordinary classroom.
Where a generation ago parents demanded—rightly—that
communities bear the cost of providing specialized education
for their offspring, they now want the further equality of having it provided within the mainstream. Children doubtless can
accommodate themselves to the disruption; witness the rough
and ready way that the retarded girl's classmates perceived
exactly what contribution she could make to their learning.

But teachers feel compelled as well to honor the egalitarian distortion that every child ought to be judged against his or her potential rather than against absolute standards. In Johnson City and elsewhere, as the *Times* noted, "Teachers set different goals for different students; some might get top grades if they learn part of the material." Consider for a moment the lesson that teaches the rest of the class. Accomplishment is not objective and standards are not fixed. The governing principles are ideology and sentiment.

If one wishes to foretell the future of a society, one should visit its public school classrooms to see what is happening now. This, more than any love of pedagogy for its own sake, has prompted me to write frequent articles for *Time,* including cover stories, about the evolving curriculum and values. Education is both the mirror and maker of modernity, reflecting the values of contemporary culture and instilling them in the succeeding generation. Schools prepare the next entrants into the work force, and the skills and attitudes those pupils absorb will determine the fate of American industry's attempts to compete in a global marketplace. Schools perpetuate the social contract, exposing children to ethnicities, priorities, beliefs, and metaphysics not found at home. Ideally, this leads them to be tolerant and comprehending toward fellow citizens, so that they can join in common cause. Schools promulgate and, in so doing, often redefine the national myth, interpreting the meaning of America's past in the light of its evolving present. Above all, schools take children at an impressionable age and teach them what to expect, or in some cases demand, from life. From what I have seen, they are learning the wrong beliefs.

There was a time, not so very long ago and still fondly remembered by most who lived through it, when schools taught discipline, self-denial, deference to one's betters, and other elitist values. Teachers had little time for encouraging students' self-expression and consumerist self-assertion because it was understood that schools were preparation for life and that very few jobs indeed offered much scope for self-expression or self-assertion. School was boot camp, not therapy. Educators tried to be aware of social problems but had no illusions of being able to solve them immediately; moreover, parents and students did not expect that. Learning was considered a social good because it would improve matters over the course of generations, not necessarily within a single lifetime. The world was bluntly realistic about this. I remember vividly from my fifties childhood a slogan that appeared on innumerable New York City bus and subway advertising cards. "Drop out of school," it read, "and they'll call you 'boy' all your life." This advice appeared without overt protest from minority leaders whose heirs would be howling if it were to be proffered now. The leaders of that era apparently understood the pedagogical values of shame and fear; uproar about individual rights and dignity would accomplish nothing of value if it effectively resulted in condoning ignorance and accelerating the dropout rate. By and large, moreover, those minority leaders recognized that people of whatever social or personal handicaps had to take responsibility for their own destinies. While awaiting a better and fairer world, we were obliged to make the most of the world we lived in.

At about the time I was passing through the schools, the educational establishment started replacing shame and fear with the cotton candy of the "social promotion"—promoting and even graduating students who had not done the necessary work and achieved the necessary proficiency because it would be too stigmatizing to leave them back or let them drop out sans diploma. One impetus for the change was the temporary but pervasive phenomenon of the Vietnam War draft. Teachers knew that flunking young men, or even giving them low grades, might literally condemn them to death. At my somewhat above average suburban high school, from which in previous years no more than sixty percent of the graduates had gone on to further education (including junior college, electricians' academy, beauty school, and the like), in my departing year of 1967 some ninety percent continued their schooling, including virtually all the boys—and I know of only one classmate who died in Vietnam.

The war ended a few years later, but the corrupting policies continued. It has been widely documented that many of our inner-city high school graduates (particularly those who can dextrously wield a basketball, football, or baseball) are unleashed upon the world barely able to read. Or spell. Or count. Or, obviously, fill out a job application, comprehend the government coverage in a worthwhile newspaper, or avert exploitation by flimflam artists. If students cannot meet the erstwhile standards of attainment, schools find it easier to lower the standards than to raise the performance.

Teachers and administrators are guided to this misplaced indulgence by at least five factors. One is the new place of schools as social worker and national nanny, providing everything from free hot lunches for the indigent to counseling and physical protection for the abused. This breeds in teachers a sense that their primary mission is to succor the young rather than instruct and assess them. Second is the increased ideological scrutiny of schools by organized minority groups, with the concomitant assumption that higher failure rates for blacks and Hispanics than for whites is a reflection of failure by the schools rather than by the students, their homes, and their communities. Third is the acceleration in the depth and scope of citizens' feelings of "entitlement," the bane of competition in so many arenas. Where a generation ago people felt entitled to a chance at education, they now feel entitled to the credential affirming that they have completed a course of study regardless of their actual mastery.

Fourth, and closely allied, is a widespread erosion in students' regard for authority and willingness to learn. George Cohen, a human-relations specialist in the White Plains, New

York, school district, calls this the "Bart Simpson syndrome." As quoted in *The New York Times,* he says of high schoolers given an assignment: "There's a disbelief that somehow they're going to be held accountable for getting it in on time. It's that attitude that drives a lot of us nuts." The *Times* adds: "The change that teachers and administrators talk about is fairly recent, and noted not just by the middle-aged but by those who are too young themselves to remember dress codes and silence-in-the-halls edicts. 'It's absolutely incredible,' said Carol Gordon Horner, an eighth-grade language arts teacher in Charlotte, North Carolina, who returned to the classroom in 1991 after a thirteen-year absence. 'Kids have a real sense of entitlement now that you didn't see before. It's almost like a make-me attitude—it's not that they won't respect you, but they won't respect you just because you're an adult. It used to be automatic. Now there's a testing mechanism that goes on constantly.' " Lillian Katz, professor of early childhood education at the University of Illinois, sees potential roots of this in a pervasive narcissism and self-congratulation urged upon children at the elementary level. In the summer 1993 issue of *American Educator,* she remarks:

A project by a first grade class in an affluent Middle Western suburb that I recently observed showed how self-esteem and narcissism can be confused. Working from copied pages prepared by the teacher, each student produced a booklet called "All About Me." The first page asked for basic information about the child's home and family. The second page was titled "what I like to eat," the third was "what I like to watch on TV," the next was "what I want for a present" and another was "where I want to go on vacation."

The booklet, like thousands of others I have encountered around the country, had no page headings such as "what I want to know more about," "what I am curious about," "what I want to solve" or even "to make."

Each page was directed toward the child's basest inner gratifications. Each topic put the child in the role of consumer—of food, entertainment, gifts, and recreation. Not once was the child asked to play the role of producer, investigator, initiator, explorer, experimenter or problem-solver.

It is perhaps this kind of literature that accounts for a poster I saw in a school entrance hall. Pictures of clapping hands surround the title "We Applaud Ourselves." While the sign's probable purpose was to help children feel good about themselves, it did so by directing their attention inward. The poster urged self-congratulation; it made no reference to possible ways of earning applause—by considering the feelings or needs of others.

Fifth and by no means least among these dispiriting trends is the careerist consideration that poor test results and high failure rates can lead to the ouster of administrators and a loss of public support for raises in teachers' salaries. It is in almost everyone's venal interest to make things look better than they are. In truth, of course, they are worse.

Even among the quasi-elite subset of high school students who go on to college, Scholastic Aptitude Test scores have been more or less steadily declining, albeit with a recent minor uptick. The average verbal score was 422 in 1992, versus 478 in 1963—even though many scholars contend that today's test is easier, having been deliberately "dumbed down." The SAT may, as alleged, have a cultural bias. It asks about things that a mainstream person ought to know but that the underclass may not yet have learned. Further, the SAT may not be the ideal test of intelligence or preparation or ability to handle college courses. Yet it *does* measure some things: vocabulary, problem-solving, reading comprehension, ability to draw logical inferences. These skills are undeniably important for college and for further life. The customary explanation for the decline in scores—the increase in numbers of deprived minority students taking the test—does not begin to account for all the difference. Granted that the low-end group might, in a more inclusive admissions era, rank rather lower than before. Why has the statistical performance of the upper-end students, the sort who go to the best colleges, also declined (albeit with a partial rebound in mathematics)? Affirmative action alone won't explain it. Indeed, at most prestigious colleges, affirmative action programs are having trouble meeting their quotas. At my alma mater, Yale, where I served on an alumni board committee concerned with admissions (which meant, for ninety percent of the discussion time, minority recruiting), I learned that as of the late 1980s, black male "yield" had fallen by half compared to the preceding decade, not only at Yale but at many of its competitors. No one was quite sure why, although explanations ranged from drugs to despair. One black Yale classmate of mine assured me, in all seriousness, that it was the result of a conscious decision by the powers that be to "throw away a whole generation of black men." Oddly, black women continued to qualify and enroll, suggesting that the problem lay within the black community rather than in white society. Hispanic students from the Southwest and California were similarly difficult to recruit, I was told, because families were reluctant to send them so far away and because, in a society that no longer encourages elitism, parents were reluctant to see one of their children get a better education and broader opportunities than the others, for fear of breaking up family unity.

Whatever the role minorities play in affecting scores—and that impact should have been fully reflected more than a decade ago, when affirmative action took sway—clearly SAT scores have declined (despite some softening of the test) because student knowledge and perspicacity have declined. Moreover, rather than face up to this decline, lobbying groups assert that the SAT discriminates against the handicapped and that the PSAT, used by the National Merit Scholarships, discriminates against women. The "proof," according to Cinthia Schuman of the National Center for Fair and Open Testing:

boys get higher scores. In fairness, girls do get higher grades. But that does not necessarily mean they are smarter. They may just be better behaved and more apt to win teachers over.

It is fashionable to blame television as the primary culprit for the overall decline in student performance, but this assertion is anti-chronological. Television played at least as pervasive a role in the childhood and adolescence of my contemporaries as it does in our children's generation (as witness the boundless popular taste for fifties and sixties TV nostalgia). Debate continues to rage about why the decline has happened (and, in some quarters where the fact is politically inconvenient, about *if* it has happened), but some of the reasons are obvious. Parents no longer teach reverence for authority and learning. Many of them arrive at teacher conferences loaded for bear, prepared to treat any shortcoming of their child's as exclusively the fault of the school—if they come at all, which is anecdotally reported to be less and less likely, as more mothers work outside the home. Students reared on *Sesame Street* expect learning to be chirpy, funny, swift-paced, and full of entertainment. They have far less patience than their forebears with such wearisome but necessary tasks as memorization. Teachers, who once viewed their work as akin to a religious vocation, are increasingly unionized and intransigent toward extra work. Too often they convey no sense to their students of school as a spiritual place, of learning as holy. School administrators and counselors now see their institutions (or are forced by community pressures to see them) as rehabilitation centers obliged to make up for the social and psychological deficiencies of some parents, the ignorance and bone idleness of others, the economic privations of others still, and the myriad unkindnesses of nature. Where schools of the fifties, particularly post-*Sputnik,* focused on stimulating the brightest, schools of today focus on bringing the backward up to speed. Often, as a matter of policy, they hinder or at least do not help the brightest to become the best they can be. In fifties educational parlance, a "special" child meant a gifted one. Now it usually means one who is severely handicapped.

Last and far from least, authors and publishers have turned the textbook business into a grand truckling to political correctness at the expense of accuracy, of perspective, and above all of challenge. As retired Cornell professor Donald Hayes has demonstrated using a computer analysis, the language difficulty of textbooks has dropped by about twenty percent during the past couple of generations. Having sampled 788 texts used between 1860 and 1992, he says, "Honors high school texts are no more difficult than an eighth grade reader was before World War II."

Perhaps the best measure of what has gone wrong is the fact, attested to by textbook authors and editors, that publishers now employ more people to censor books for content that might offend any organized lobbying group than they do to check the correctness of facts. From a business point of view, that makes sense. A book is far more apt to be struck off a purchase order because it contains terminology or vignettes that irritate the hypersensitive than because it is erroneous.

The results are chilling. When it came time to vote on new textbooks for use in Texas schools during the 1992–93 academic year, one member of the state Board of Education wondered aloud whether the planned $20.2 million expenditure was really quite wise. One of the books scheduled for adoption, she pointed out, informed children that the United States had settled its conflict in Korea by "using the bomb." This apparent reference to nonexistent nuclear warfare was just one of 231 factual errors cited by conservative critics whose deeper objections are to galloping feminism and multiculturalism but who are given ammunition against such volumes by their cheerful disregard for precise fact. Among other prominent errors in the texts were assertions that Robert Francis Kennedy and Martin Luther King, Jr., were assassinated during the Republican presidency of Richard Nixon rather than the Democratic regime of his predecessor, Lyndon Johnson, and that George Bush defeated Michael Dukakis in the election of 1989 rather than 1988—a calendar howler that ought to have jumped out at any author, editor, copy editor, or fact checker who ever took an elementary school civics course about our quadrennial system. For pointing this out, the school board member was criticized by some of her colleagues for allegedly playing politics and by others, including some scholars, for trivializing the more important quest for a politically correct view of the sins of conquest with a "nit-picking" emphasis on fact.

This was not an isolated incident, moreover. In a harrowing article called "The Other Crisis in American Education" in the November 1991 *Atlantic Monthly,* Professor Daniel J. Singal surveys statistically and anecdotally the pervasive historical ignorance of even that superior slice of the high school population that manages to go to prestigious colleges. "I will never forget two unusually capable juniors," he recalls, "one of whom was a star political-science major, who came to my office a few years ago to ask what was this thing called the New Deal. I had made reference to it during a lecture, on the assumption that everyone would be well acquainted with Franklin Roosevelt's domestic program, but I was wrong: the two students had checked with their friends, and none of them had heard of the New Deal either. Another junior recently asked me to help him pick a twentieth-century American novelist on whom to write a term paper. He had heard vaguely of F. Scott Fitzgerald and Ernest Hemingway, but did not recognize the names of Sinclair Lewis, John Dos Passos, Norman Mailer, William Styron and Saul Bellow." Singal goes on to quote Paula Fass, a professor of history at the University of California at Berkeley, to the effect that college sophomores and juniors cannot distinguish between the American Revolution and the Civil War, "but rather see them as two big events that happened way back in the past." He quotes Harvard professor of English Alan Heimert as saying of his presumably top-drawer students: "They are aware that someone oppressed someone else, but they aren't sure exactly what took place and they have no idea of the order in which it happened."

More ignorance is being brewed every minute. The books that Texas caviled at were offered for sale, and doubtless taken up, in some less vigilant jurisdictions. Their errors were at least apparently innocent. According to a leading figure in textbook publishing, some of the most outrageous misstatements in textbooks are written in deliberately to placate pressure groups, some of whose ideological partisans are actually in the publishers' employ—most notably ardent feminists, whom this executive describes as "the most relentless, overall the worst." The person in question is sufficiently fearful of retaliation not to want to be identified by name, age, gender, or even the citation of any specific example.

Another conspicuous example of this kowtowing is the development of "Afrocentric" curricula. There is nothing wrong with teaching children a lot more about Africa than we learned in my youth. If anything, the need is even greater for white children, who are less apt to hear anything about African culture and contributions at home. But many Afrocentric texts assert things about the African past that are dubious or outright false, in the name of enhancing black children's self-esteem and sense of rightful participation in the larger culture, while white textbook publishers and school boards condescendingly look the other way. These implausibilities will be discussed in a later chapter; it is worth noting two in passing here. First is the prevalent claim that ancient Egypt was a "black" civilization. It was unquestionably a multiracial one, with a ruling class drawn from black Nubians, brown Nile Delta natives, and white Macedonian Greeks, among others. Cleopatra was certainly a lot darker than her grandest impersonator, Elizabeth Taylor. But the Egyptians neither thought of themselves as African in the modern sense—they were, if anything, a Middle Eastern power—nor viewed themselves as ethnically bonded to the hundreds if not thousands of sub-Saharan tribes, many of whom they had never encountered. The second dubious assertion is that Arabian number theory, astronomy, and other early science derived from Africa; usually this is accompanied by an ancillary assertion that white people have connived for centuries to cover up this heritage, to promote submission to slavery and subsequent political and economic domination. Quite apart from the thinness, to put it politely, of evidence supporting this claim, the problem is how to explain the almost total lack of progress in science, technology, hygiene, and medicine among later African peoples. If they had such a great head start, what does it say about their culture that it all drifted away? Any attempt to answer this question just leads to more attitudinizing about conspiracy and more outlandish attempts to exaggerate or fabricate African achievements.

What is the result of such education? It breeds children who are resentful, hostile, even paranoid. It fosters a pseudo-racial pride not far removed from hatred. And it makes young people suspicious for life of the mainstream sources of information that they need to compete in the marketplace. The columnist George Will likes to quote a line that he says Cardinal Wolsey uttered about Henry VIII: "Be very, very careful what you put into that head, because you will never, ever get it out." The relevance of that description is not limited to kings. Things we learn when young remain to almost all of us the deepest truths we know throughout life. Even in the face of overwhelming evidence, we are hardly ever ready to accept that they are, and always were, falsehoods.

That is why it is wicked for the state of New York to mandate that children be taught that one of the two main sources of ideas for the United States Constitution was the organizing pact of the Iroquois Indian nation. This intellectual debt was not, to say the least, profusely acknowledged by the Founding Fathers. It is a latter-day scholarly discovery (or should we say invention?), promoted by the same sort of special pleader who will tell you in the next breath how the pioneer white man hated, cheated, and murdered the red man, never finding anything of value in his culture. Well, which is it? Did we "invaders" scorn the "natives" as beneath contempt, or did we so admire their sagacity that we modeled our government on theirs? And if the latter, then how can one account for the ferocity of our wars of conquest and extirpation? No other state teaches this particular balderdash, so far as I have been able to discover, presumably because no other state government faces sufficiently sizable and efficacious lobbying efforts by descendants of the Iroquois tribe.

The portrayal of the "First Americans"—or should we follow the hyphenate craze and call them Siberian-Americans?— is one of the most conspicuous areas in which fact has been transmuted to suit political necessity. Where textbooks once elucidated Frederick Turner's concept of Manifest Destiny, they now wallow in guilt. The prevailing view was invoked sympathetically by Alan Brinkley of Columbia University, writing for *The New York Times Book Review:* "Western American history, transformed by a new generation of energetic revisionist scholars, is staging a vigorous and important revival. No other region has had so long and intensive experience of racial and ethnic diversity; no other place displays the imprint of multiculturalism more clearly."

Other scholars take a dimmer view of the values being promulgated in textbooks and treatises. The distinguished Yale historian C. Vann Woodward has summed up the brave new world of contemporary study this way:

The new guilt is different. It is something congenital, inherent, intrinsic, collective, something possibly inexpiable, and probably ineradicable. The first English settlers, south as well as north, arrived with it in their hearts, and they never should have come in the first place. Invasion was their initial offense. The pattern of collective rapacity and inhuman cruelty to darker peoples that characterized their westward conquests of the Pacific shores and on across the ocean ever westward through Asia is seen as existing from the very outset. From this point of view the line of precedents stretched from the slaughter of braves in the Pequot War of 1637 on for three centuries and more to Lieutenant Calley at My Lai, with little more than changes in the technology of annihilation. Thus interpreted, American history becomes primarily a history of oppression, and the focus is upon the oppressed. . . . The exercise of defining national (or racial) character in terms of guilt attributed takes on some peculiar traits in the American instance. It might be called, in a sense, unilateral. In most instances, that is, the guilt is to all appearances unshared, the offenses incurring it unprovoked, unique and confined to the dominant group. If other nations have perpetrated comparable or worse offenses against their native population, black slaves and freedmen, racial minorities, neighboring countries, or remote Asian or African cultures, the opportunities for perspective by comparing the magnitude of the offenses and the number of casualties are passed over. Those American offenses that were confined to intraracial conflict also go largely unremarked. . . . This teaching recalls by contrast the recent time when we were taught that America "held up a lamp" of hope to Asia and Africa. . . . Neither the old myth of innocence nor the self-therapy of collective guilt has proved to be of much help to Americans with their problems.

The faddish environmental extremism among the young makes the promulgation of white guilt and Siberian-American virtue all the more popular, because the latter people are understood (and to a degree misunderstood) to have had a zookeeper reverence for the land and its creatures. There are good reasons to temper this view. Evan Connell, in his anti-Custer biography *Son of the Morning Star,* documents how Indians were just as apt as whites to kill buffalo without making full use of their meat, hides, hooves, and so on. In the case of Plains Indians, the buffalo nonpareil was the nose. The rest was often left to rot. The white men were more destructive because they were more numerous and better equipped, not because they had different souls.

This is not, of course, the sort of nuance one will find in a textbook. The noble savage of my youth is still noble, but savage no more.

One amusing irony is that celebrating Indians raises ticklish political questions among another pressure cadre, the feminists. The Indians had a gender-specific social structure. Women were not warriors or chiefs or medicine men (the very name implies the exclusion). Women had a clearly subordinate role, one that feminists wish away because it makes it hard to justify their reverence for the Indians' other fine qualities (their nonwhiteness, their non-Europeanness, their nontechnological culture, their relative lack of capitalism).

The Social Studies Review, a publication of the liberal but traditionally oriented American Textbook Council, contrasts two passages about American Indian life in its spring 1993 issue. The passage from a fifth-grade text used during the 1950s reads:

Now we see, standing just outside the doorway, the Chippewa mother. She is wearing a buckskin shirt which reaches to her toes. On her feet are moccasins, and about her shoulders a garment much like a shawl. Her small black eyes look out of a broad brown face. The hair of this Indian woman is black and straight and coarse. Just now it is drawn into an untidy mop at the back of her head. . . .

Indian women worked hard. With the help of the girls, they gathered all the wood for the fires. The women skinned and cleaned the game that was brought in by the hunters. They dressed the skins, tanned them, and cut and sewed all the clothing for the family. The Indian women tended the fields of corn and squash and beans. Of course, they carried the water and took care of the children and cooked all the meals.

The Indian men never helped their wives with the work around the wigwams. They would have felt it a disgrace to help with the work of the squaws. . . . *(Squaw* is a word that means Indian woman.) [Squaws] loved their children, just as white mothers do. They taught their daughters how to take care of a wigwam and helped their sons to become brave warriors.

The writing is vivid, the sense of daily life powerfully evoked, the women honorably portrayed as hardworking and productive. There may be a marginal insensitivity in the sentence about mothers loving their children. But we should remember that this was written in the heyday of the movie and TV western, which typically depicted Indians as unfeeling brutes with scant regard for life. In the context of its times, this passage embodied decency. By the standards of contemporary advocates, however, the objectionable part is the almost certainly true statement that men would have felt themselves disgraced to take part in domestic women's work. I cannot say for sure that this was true of bygone Indians. It is emphatically true today of third world cultures I have observed firsthand in Latin America, Africa, the subcontinent, and the Middle East. Contemporary American women, however, frequently believe that the best way to alter the present and future to their liking is to reconceive the past. Hence the assertion in *United States and Its Neighbors,* the largest-selling history in the nation's elementary schools: "In spite of the importance of warriors, women played a major role in Iroquois life. They could not be priests or healers, but it was the women who decided which men would be chiefs." This statement seems to be more true than false—but it also, troublingly, seems to be more widely viewed as true today than it was forty years ago. What has changed, Iroquois history or classroom sensibilities? The text's ideological cousin, *American Voices,* aimed at high school students, takes the women's lib line so far that it is, says the Textbook Council, "less versed in evidence than aligned to contemporary feminist politics and perspectives." Perhaps not incidentally, the prose is dogmatic and devoid of color. Consider the following:

First, [North American native] families were organized along kinship lines, meaning that family membership was defined by blood connection. In many Native American societies, family connections were matrilineal, that is, made through the female line. A typical family thus consisted of an old woman, her daughters with their husbands and children, and her unmarried granddaughters and grandsons. When a son or grandson married, he moved from this female-headed household to one headed by the female leader of his wife's family. Women also controlled divorce. If a woman wanted a divorce, she simply set her husband's possessions outside their dwelling door. Families were joined in clans, again defined by kinship ties.

Second, the division of labor within Indian societies most frequently set women in charge of child care and cultivation or agriculture. The men were responsible for activities in which child care would be a burden, such as hunting, trading, and fighting.

Politically, women's roles and status varied from culture to culture. Women were more likely to assume leadership roles among the agricultural peoples than among nomadic hunters. In addition, in many cases in which women did not become village chiefs, they still exercised substantial political power. For example, in Iroquois villages, when selected men sat in a circle to discuss and make decisions, the senior women of the village stood behind them, lobbying and instructing the men. In addition, the elder women named the male village chiefs to their positions.

There is something endearingly funny in the attempt to portray as influential, and validating of women, a behind-the-scenes role exactly akin to what feminists reject today. Even more sweetly crackers is the underlying notion that the one vital and surpassing question to ask about this or any culture is what status it gave women. And when the answer is abundantly clear—they had no real role in hunting, war, or religion, the defining aspects of their society—it is engagingly disingenuous to pretend that the society was defined instead by crop-planting and divorce. The smiles die on one's lips, however, when one realizes that this is absolutely typical of what the next generation is being taught to think. I am by no means endorsing a sexist society. I grew up in a female-headed household and am used to female authority. It put food on my plate. But I want the next generation to be able to face facts, to accept moral complexity in every sort of society, and to see the truth clearly, without politically motivated self-delusion. Admire the Indians if they embodied values you cherish. But don't reinvent their culture, or anyone else's, to suit your need for emotional black and white.

The same tormented thinking comes from other ethnic groups. African American parents, offended by the use of the word "nigger"—however historically accurate and however righteously meant—have succeeded intermittently in getting *The Adventures of Huckleberry Finn* excluded (we dare not say blacklisted) from school reading lists. This dates to at least 1957, when the book was banned for a time from New York City schools. More recently, the fatuous case against this potent indictment of slavery has been made in places as diverse as Houston, rural Pennsylvania, and the Washington, D.C., suburbs of Fairfax County, Virginia. The arguments are tribal and anti-intellectual: that no white writer of Mark Twain's era can be trusted to speak to the black experience; that painful reminders of the past only diminish black children now; that Nigger Jim is too ill educated and submissive to serve as a role model.

Mexican-Americans have had some similar success in demanding that the war of 1847 be taught as an American invasion and that the massacre at the Alamo be seen as a morally neutral standoff between patriots of two equally valid sides. Linda K. Salvucci, an associate professor of history at Trinity University in San Antonio, Texas, asserts in the fall 1992 issue of *The Public Historian:*

Four newly adopted titles for eighth-grade use offer dramatically improved treatment of multilateral and minority issues, particularly those pertaining to Mexico, Mexicans, and Mexican Americans. This is a significant development, since these U.S. history books present, more by default than design, the fullest and most widely disseminated images of Mexico and its peoples to American high-school students.

One textbook, Mason et al.'s *The History of the United States,* stands out for its distinctive organization. While the other three eighth-grade textbooks used in Texas divide up their coverage of the Mexican War for Independence, early Anglo settlement in Texas, the Texas Revolution, and the battle of the Alamo into separate chapters with different, apparently larger concerns, *The History of the United States* devotes an entire chapter to "Changes in Spanish-Speaking North America, 1810–1836." The three sections deal with "Mexican Independence," "Changes on the Borderlands," and "The Texas Revolution" respectively, weaving these topics together in an integrated, sustained, and comprehensive way.

In the past, the lack of informed and thoughtful discussion extended to another sensitive topic in bilateral continental relations, the Mexican War, known to Mexicans as the "War of 1847" or the "American Invasion." The older textbooks used to provide rather jingoist accounts of the fighting, placing it approvingly in the context of Manifest Destiny. By 1986, a few authors pointed out that there was substantial disagreement about the war in U.S. political circles. The newly approved books demonstrate much more awareness of the magnitude of this war, not only as a formative experience for Americans but also as an event that has deeply affected the Mexican psyche, influencing the relationship between the two countries even to this day.

Much more extreme critics than the self-described "moderate" Salvucci have also lobbied for textbook celebration of the glories of the purportedly sophisticated Meso-American civilization, sidestepping the awkward question as to why, if this culture was so advanced, it did not journey to and conquer Europe or at least successfully fight off the arrivistes on its own home turf. To say that there was some sort of sophisticated culture in the pre-Columbian Americas ought to be enough. It is a pretense to assert full equivalence between the easily vanquished and their conquerors. To be sure, there are scholars of some standing who assert that the real source of European triumph was disease. One prize-winning Canadian, Ronald Wright, writing in London's *TLS* (*Times Literary Supplement*), contends that in no case did Europeans prevail over indigenous rulers until at least half the native population had been stricken by some Eurogenic epidemic. One wonders how he can know this; native record-keeping in time of plague is notoriously sketchy, and even European record-keeping can scarcely have met modern statistical standards. In any case, this assertion does not explain away the triumph of Europeans. They are presumably just as vulnerable to infection from the other side (or are natives so virtuous that they are germ free?). And they were conducting military maneuvers in limited forces, with renewed supplies and troop reinforcements many thousands of miles, and therefore months or years, distant.

The assault against the dead white European male tradition in colleges has been widely publicized. But the related onslaught in elementary and secondary schools has gone largely unremarked. What ordinary, unsuspecting middle-aged adult would guess, for example, that only forty-four percent of the nation's high school students will even take a world history course before graduation, let alone that such a course will almost certainly pay far more attention to the sins of colonialism than to the failures of Marxism, and will in all likelihood represent the most important advance in human history, the arrival of Europeans to conquer and civilize North America, as a moral tragedy beyond reckoning?

As Arthur Schlesinger, Jr., argues in his 1991 lament *The Disuniting of America:* "Let us by all means teach black history, African history, women's history, Hispanic history, Asian history. But let us teach them as history, not as filiopietistic commemoration. The purpose of history is to promote not group self-esteem, but understanding of the world and the past, dispassionate analysis, judgment and perspective, respect for divergent cultures and traditions, and unflinching protection for those unifying ideas of tolerance, democracy, and human rights that make free historical inquiry possible."

The egalitarian distortion of *what* is taught (and, just as important, what is not taught) is only half of what is wrong with our schools. The other half is the egalitarian distortion of *how* things are taught. Far from providing enrichment, stimulus, and incentive to the brightest—the natural future leadership cadre—schools are increasingly questioning the moral legitimacy of ability grouping and fretting about whether the mediocrities are being developed to their full potential. A chilling example is under discussion in Montclair, New Jersey, a relatively prosperous multiracial suburb of New York City. In place of five versions of the high school course in world literature and mythology, structured to be of varying difficulty depending upon the caliber of the students, the English department proposes to have just one curriculum for everybody. Each section would be hand picked to be balanced, with quotas for race, sex, and talent. One explanation for the change: the school superintendent's assertion that high-ability black students tend not to choose challenging curricula when the fellow students are primarily white. Does this "educator" genuinely think that shielding students from competition will prepare them for the adult world and the rawly combative global economy? Another explanation, frankly ideological, comes from the English department chairman, who says, "I don't think that in a democratic society we should have classism." Montclair is not alone in clashing over ability grouping. While about eighty percent of high schools and sixty percent of elementary schools in the United States still practice some form of it, the numbers are reported to be dropping.

In November 1993, *The New York Times* reported that many such programs entail only two to three hours a week, and added, quoting a report by the U.S. Department of Education, "Few if any publishers produce textbooks aimed at above average students." In terms of financial commitment, the DOE report said, only two cents out of every hundred dollars spent on education for kindergarten through grade twelve is for support of special programs for the talented, and even these modest programs are among the first to go during rounds of budget-cutting. The results are predictable, the report added. As the *Times* phrased it: "Compared with top students in other industrialized countries, American students perform poorly on international tests, are offered a less rigorous curriculum, read fewer demanding books, do less homework and enter the work force or postsecondary school less prepared." As the report's researchers noted, one test of nine-year-olds and thirteen-year-olds from twenty industrial nations ranked the American students near the bottom in math and science. Chillingly, when asked how they thought they had performed, American students were confident that they had come out on top, while Korean children, who vastly outperformed them, assumed themselves to be near the bottom.

The most disturbing aspect of the report, however, was that despite all this evidence of failure, the authors *opposed* ability grouping, known as "tracking," seemingly on egalitarian ideological grounds. Explained primary author Pat O'Connell Ross, director of the federally funded Javits Gifted and Talented Education Center: "One of the major messages is that all kids need to be performing at higher levels." Thus, she explained, she believes the bright need to mingle with other students in order to spur the learning of their less gifted contemporaries.

When New York City announced the opening of thirty-seven new, smaller high schools, most with specialized "themes," for the fall of 1993, it specifically forbade "creaming" of the ablest students, even if the new curricula represented what they most wanted to study and even if they might benefit by being grouped together. Not all the new high schools were neutrally academic, of course. Among them were a Coalition School for Social Change, a High School for Leadership and Public Service, an Urban Peace Academy, a Local 1199 (!) School for Social Change, a Brooklyn School for Global Citizenship, a Benjamin Banneker Academy for Community Development, two East Brooklyn Congregations High Schools for Public Service, an El Puente Academy for Peace and Justice, a Thurgood Marshall Academy for Learning and Social Change, and a Middle College High School at Medgar Evers College—but nothing, of course, dedicated to a classical curriculum.

Products of ability grouping programs—and I should admit that I am one myself—tend to favor them, perhaps because of some residual feeling of prestige, perhaps because they actually do benefit the gifted students on whom society ought to focus. In Brockton, Massachusetts, graduates of the school system's tracking program organized their own 1992 reunion, traveling in some cases considerable distances at their own expense, when the city was pondering whether to dismantle the curriculum in favor of a unified and egalitarian education.

In an anonymous poll that they conducted themselves, fifty-six percent favored retaining the full-day tracking program and another ten percent favored partial tracking, subject by subject. Some thirty-one percent favored enrichment programs of extra or harder work within the regular classroom, a form of tracking without physical separation. Only thirteen percent favored total abolition of the special curriculum, and many of those did so on political grounds rather than on the basis of having failed to benefit. The bulk of the respondents were in mid-career, long enough removed from school that they had more substantial and much more recent attainments on which to base self-pride. In citing positive aspects of the Brockton curriculum, no respondent mentioned prestige or privilege; instead, they cited self-confidence (sixteen percent), creativity (eighteen percent), intellectual challenge (eighteen percent), and, in lesser proportions, competition, independence, friendship, and superior teaching. Among the negative aspects they cited, three fifths of the tally seemingly reflected other people's resentment of their privilege: social isolation (forty-three percent), underdevelopment of social skills (eight percent), and snobbery (nine percent).

No educational researcher has convincingly demonstrated that tracking or ability grouping has adverse intellectual impact upon able students. Indeed, most scholars readily concede that the gifted students do better when challenged to keep up with each other. The fretting is about what happens to average and subpar students, which is a humane concern but a misplaced one. As Charles Murray of the American Enterprise Institute wrote last year, "The real failure in U.S. schools for the average and below-average students has been in socializing them to adult behavior. This training in how to be a good worker was especially important for children who grew up in disorganized homes. In many schools, particularly those in urban areas, this socializing function no longer exists. How can it be restored? Rethinking student rights would be a start." Murray went on to argue: "Education has gone downhill academically for the gifted. Achievement among the best students fell substantially during the 1960s and 1970s. Their math scores recovered somewhat during the 1980s but their verbal scores did not. This means that deterioration has been most pronounced in the reasoning and analytic skills crucial to the development of intellectual creativity and judgment. Our best students may go to college in large numbers, but they arrive much more poorly developed than their counterparts of thirty years ago. Meanwhile, programs for the gifted languish or disappear altogether." His prescription: "Pay more attention to the education of the thin layer of gifted who, like it or not, will determine whether we remain the world's pre-eminent nation in the twenty-first century."

Whatever attitude schools take toward the relative importance of the gifted and the sluggish, there are sharp limits to what they can do. As Joel N. Shurkin reports in his 1992 book about a groundbreaking Stanford University study that followed the gifted through life, starting in 1922:

Professor Lewis M. Terman demonstrated that success, if not intelligence, ran in families. Whether it was genetic or environmental or, more likely, both is impossible to divine from his study. Unquestionably, however, certain families primed their children for success in life and others sent them off with a handicap. The single greatest determinant of success was education. The homes of the most successful child subjects typically had at least a five-hundred-book library. Good grades and extracurricular activities were thought of as a norm and were actively encouraged. In these families, whether a son or, in most cases, a daughter should go to college probably was never an issue, even when paying for it was. Families were important in other ways. The Terman researchers found that the families of most of the highly successful subjects were close and affectionate and the role of the father was surprisingly strong. The fathers were not passive and they did not leave child-rearing exclusively to the mother. Success was expected.

In short, if you wish to produce an elite, you must live by elite values. Neither schools nor their constituents, alas, are prepared these days to embrace that reality. Instead, it is seen as enough, as was the case in Montclair, to revile an emphasis on the talented as "elitist"—as though the mere invocation of the word should be enough to taint the thought and so end the debate. The very essence of school is elitism. Schools exist to teach, to test, to rank hierarchically, to promote the idea that knowing and understanding more is better than knowing and understanding less. Education is elitist. Civilization is elitist. Egalitarianism celebrates the blissful ignorance of the Garden of Eden, where there were no Newtons to perceive the constructive use of an apple.

The underexamined problems in our elementary and secondary schools go far beyond some teachers' desires to inculcate egalitarian values or to protest against the existence of a snobbish adult elite that their occupation has almost always been excluded from. The core issue is our loss of faith in the right of every individual to fulfill his potential, stretch his talent, and chart his own course. We used to tell our schools to give children the capacity to adapt to, and in the best case to help navigate, an unknowable future. We now subordinate their fate to the political ambitions of adults more concerned with the present and past. Our schools always had an ideological bent to their education. These days they too often have a mere educational bent to their central mission of ideology.

THREE

Affirmative Confusion

"Instead of a transformative nation with an identity all its own, America increasingly sees itself as preservative of old identities. Instead of a nation composed of individuals making their own free choices, America increasingly sees itself as composed of groups more or less indelible in their ethnic character. The national ideal had once been *e pluribus unum*. Are we now to belittle *unum* and glorify *pluribus*? Will the center hold? Or will the melting pot yield to the Tower of Babel?"

— ARTHUR SCHLESINGER, JR., *The Disuniting of America*

THE MOST BASIC FACT of American life is this: Sometime within the next fifty or so years, non-Hispanic white people will become demographically just another minority group. They will be collectively outnumbered by Hispanics of all races, blacks, Asians, Indians (in both vernacular meanings), and assorted other ethnic groups not associated with western Europe. Within the work force, this shift to a no-majority America will happen substantially sooner. Whites already tend to be older than other ethnic groups and to reproduce less prolifically. Moreover, immigration, legal and otherwise, is bringing in a disproportionate share of Hispanics and nonwhites. Among the school age population, the new America is already showing itself. By 1990, non-Hispanic whites accounted for less than half of public school enrollment, grades kindergarten through twelve, in the entire state of California. The same will be true in New York State a few years hence, with Texas and Florida, among other places, poised to follow soon after.

This ethnic evolution provides the underlying significance to the national debate over multiculturalism. The pressure for change in how America defines itself is philosophical and ideological, but it is above all political in the most basic way. The new arrivals at the table want to reslice the pie. While some opponents of the new order are genuinely concerned with the preservation of intellectual traditions and competitive values, many others are symbolically protesting the change in America's face and character. They want to ensure the longevity of a nation resembling the one they grew up in. To them, fuss and feathers about the place of Plato in the syllabuses of the better colleges is all well and good for getting the adrenaline racing in the bloodstream of traditionalists. They see sincere reasons to protest the manipulation of the elementary and secondary school curriculum. They do not wish to celebrate primitive cultures or to castigate the leadership cadres of the past for brutalities wholly normal for those times.

But they also feel an ethnic anxiety uncomfortably close to racism. During the later 1970s, evangelist-politician Pat Robertson built a following for his *The 700 Club* that eventually launched him into a 1988 presidential campaign and ongoing political manipulations far afield of his Virginia headquarters. (For example, he put up a slate of endorsed candidates during New York City's 1993 school board elections and, appallingly, got quite a few of them elected.) While Robertson tends to speak in more discreet code language now, in earlier days he preached that a vital reason to oppose abortion was racial power. In the absence of sufficient white fecundity, he warned on air, within a couple of generations the majority of the United States population would derive from Asia, Africa, and Latin America and would "lack our Anglo-Saxon heritage and values." Many of his loyal constituents heard rhetoric like that back then and are still hearing it in their mind's ears now.

Robertson is not, alas, a lone nut preaching in the wilderness. When I wrote a 1990 cover story for *Time* laying out the demographic facts of the American future and sketching some of the implications—illustrated by a cover image of the American flag in browns and yellows, emblazoned with the words "America's changing colors"—readers sent in more than a thousand letters. About half were fiercely disapproving. They divided more or less equally between people who favored this change in America but feared that we would slow it by calling attention to it and people who opposed the change and worried that we would legitimize it by paying it notice. The latter group included not a few who implied that a nonwhite

America could not be a "real" America. The two sides agreed on nothing except the worrisome preference for silence over open debate—and, of course, the inescapable notion that a multiracial America will be very different from a white-dominated one.

Plenty of nonracists, like Arthur Schlesinger, Jr., as quoted above, are fretful over the impact of the ethnic evolution. They recognize that a different racial identity will to a considerable degree redefine the nation's future. At the core of the many battles over multiculturalism is the deeper and emotionally more explosive reality that racial change is already redefining the nation's past. Traditional judgments about what America has meant to its own people and to the world get radically altered when someone new does the interpreting, from a different perspective and often with a chip on the shoulder. Historians and cultural scholars who see the American experience as the world's most successful experiment in governance and creativity are being jostled aside by those with a grudge against the past and present. Some are feminists, some are gay liberationists, and not a few are unregenerate Marxists who refuse to regard the breakup of the Soviet empire as any kind of definitive judgment on the intellectual bankruptcy of socialist egalitarianism.

The most potent threats, however, come from thinkers with a racial agenda. Women's rights and gay rights can be integrated within the American mainstream, and to an astonishing degree already have been. Racial scholars, however, often seek not to expand traditional American values but to supplant them. As Schlesinger so deftly points out, there used to be something called Americanism to which, liberals thought, anyone of any ethnicity ought to be welcome. Now the definition of Americanism is argued to be exactly equivalent to the sum total of the ancestral languages, cultures, religions, beliefs, intuitions, totems, and taboos of all the individuals living within the country, legally or not. They do not have to become American. Instead, America must redefine itself to embrace them. If American values and customs collide with theirs, then the American tradition must give way to accommodating the new ethnic pluralism, sans unity. The once-proud phrase "melting pot" is now viewed as an expression not of ethnic advancement, but of quislinglike capitulation. As conservative an institution as Chemical Bank distributed in 1993 a flier about a high school debate program it was sponsoring that admiringly quoted a New Utrecht High School student as saying, "In a culturally diverse society, everybody belongs. The melting pot is an absolute contradiction to what American democracy stands for." Set against that was a contrary view from a student at Midwood High in Brooklyn. But the anti–melting pot words were featured first and foremost, and they expressed misguided views that no one would have touted a generation ago.

This anti-assimilation posture would, if taken seriously, lead to an ungovernably fissile nation. Fortunately, the vast majority of new arrivals and, for that matter, the vast majority of such incompletely assimilated groups as African Americans still see both the practical value of participating in the mainstream and the spiritual satisfaction of plunging into patriotism. In any case, racial inclusion in and of itself need not pose any threat to elitist standards. Inclusion as defined in the era of the melting pot was egalitarian only in the positive sense of giving everyone a chance.

In the seamy world of practical politics, however, multiculturalism promotes quotas over competition, allocation of resources over attainment of them, a cabinet that "looks like America" over one that has sufficient background not to require on-the-job training. If some multicultural extremists had their way, the United States would do business in the fashion of Malaysia, where advancement of the backward native population was ensured by the simple legal expedient of requiring that every executive hired from other races would have to be matched, one for one, by an executive from the protected group, regardless of talent or credentials. That is affirmative action at its crudest. But it is not all that far removed from the way things work in many American institutions. Nor is it entirely different from the views that nearly got Lani Guinier the post as President Clinton's civil rights chief in the justice department. She argued that protecting minority rights may be close to meaningless if the minority, as a permanent and distinct minority, never becomes part of a coalition shaping public policy. In such circumstances, she suggested, open competition might not be enough. Special advantages might have to be conferred.

That is the dilemma for American multiculturalists. On the one hand, they want all heritages and groups to be equal. On the other hand, like Orwell's pigs, they want some to be more equal than others. Scholarly multiculturalism, with its emphasis on cruelty and oppression in the past, is in effect the propaganda arm of affirmative action and other political quota plans.

One salient example of this link is multiculturalism's ritual, buzz-word emphasis on the "voices" of the formerly dispossessed. In early 1993, New York's Hunter College—a public institution that for decades served its working-class clientele by demanding that they meet rigorous and traditional academic standards—shifted to a curriculum explicitly based on this theme. All incoming freshmen would henceforth be required to take twelve credit hours (about a third of their academic course load) from among the four categories of European cultures, non-European cultures, American studies, and women's studies and sexual orientation (the latter two, revealingly, grouped under one rubric). The college's president at the time, Paul Le Clerc, explained that he was "motivated by a belief that any college in a melting-pot city like New York would be remiss in its academic duty if it did not expose students to the diverse voices of women, minority group members and foreign cultures." With minor variations in wording, this sentence could have been uttered by countless heads of changing academic institutions.

On one level, the rhetoric is reminiscent of the words of the Bush-era appointee to the "glass ceiling" commission who said her foremost task was to accumulate "stories." It is a tenet in many of the more politically charged circles of multiculturalism that the "voices" are not to be examined too closely, certainly not subjected to analytic scrutiny, but rather are to be respected as pure cultural artifacts whose very importance lies in their lack of intermediation with conventional hierarchical elitist culture. This emphasis on the testimonial element is evocative of black churches and of women's empowerment sessions. *What is most important is the act of speaking, not what is being said.* It goes without saying that this posture is profoundly anti-intellectual and anti-rational. It provides multiculturalists a pedagogical and cultural basis for the argument that jobs and other positions of responsibility ought to be apportioned by gender and ethnicity rather than credentials or performance. In the civil service as in the classroom, the voices of the previously unheard are presumed to legitimize things merely by their testimonial presence.

There are, it should be noted, a few scholars who think that the brouhaha over multiculturalism and, for that matter, ethnic diversity is vastly oversold. Louis Menand, professor of English at New York City's Queens College, which has adopted a curriculum almost as politically correct as Hunter's, argues: "The belief that the United States is becoming more racially and culturally diversified, more like a mosaic and less like a can of mixed paint, is not supported by any statistics that I am aware of. A much smaller percentage of the population is foreign-born than was the case sixty or seventy years ago; the rate of interracial marriage has increased dramatically. Insofar as multiculturalism means genuine diversity, the United States is becoming not more multicultural but less. When the whole culture is self-consciously diverse, diversity has disappeared. Real diversity is what the United States used to have—when women and men, black and white Americans, Christians and Jews, gays and straights, and the various ethnic communities of recent immigrant groups led, culturally, largely segregated lives. Assimilation does not come from suppressing difference; it comes from mainstreaming it."

The rhetoric is compelling, the argument offbeat. But of course it has very little to do with the world most Americans perceive themselves as living in, and nothing whatever to do with the political dynamic of the present moment.

American multiculturalism of the present day embraces six basic elements that impinge to varying degrees on elitism. First is the unexamined notion that "fair" competition would automatically result in demographically proportional sharing of society's rewards, and that any deviation from such sharing is ipso facto proof of unfairness. Second is the notion of the equivalency of cultures. Third is a generalized skepticism toward, if not outright rejection of, the European heritage responsible for most of mankind's freedom and medical and material progress. Fourth is a disbelief in the value of linguistic standardization, and thus a validation both of the multigenerational preservation of Spanish as the primary tongue in growing parts of this country and also of the glorification of substandard, subliterate speech as authentic dialect or idiom ("black English"). Fifth is the wicked idea that drug dealing, gang crime, violence, and retreat from schools and learning should be regarded as natural, sensible, valid responses among the urban poor to the difficulty of their situation. Sixth is the sickeningly prevalent notion among young urban blacks that speaking standard English, getting good grades in school, and succeeding amounts to "acting white"—an equation of blackness with ignorant failure that is more racially suppressive than anything ever spoken by the Ku Klux Klan.

As this list above implies, the troublesome aspect of multiculturalism is not the opening of "our Anglo-Saxon heritage and values" to the recognition of other achievements. It is the systematic validation of black failure and Hispanic racial isolation, accompanied by a rationale that forbids polite society from labeling those things as what they are. Yes, America is multicultural. Yes, the openness of our borders makes us vulnerable to Bosnian or Islamic terrorists, Taiwanese or Pakistani assassins. But we can learn to live with that, even in a media age that whips up instant hysteria over essentially isolated incidents. And we can surely accommodate diverse groups.

No culture is more distinctly non-European than the major cultures of East Asia. Yet people of Asian stock readily adapt to the free market economy and the open competition for educational opportunities—so successfully, in fact, that the University of California at Berkeley has all but admitted it imposed a cap on the numbers of Asian-descent students admitted. Similar charges have been made against the Massachusetts Institute of Technology. The problem at nearly all prestigious colleges is not, as it is with blacks or Hispanics, recruiting sufficient numbers of Asians. The problem is to keep the Asians from crowding out the less accomplished children of donation-minded white alumni. The leadership sector of American society often asks in private why blacks and Hispanics cannot perform as Asians do. It is politically unacceptable—it would surely eliminate one from any job requiring legislative confirmation—to ask the same question out loud. This is because the question has only four possible answers: the Asians are inherently, i.e., genetically, superior; the Asian communities teach their people better values; the Asians are individually more ready to work hard, make sacrifices, and defer gratification; or the Asians are just not victims, in the way that blacks are, of the entrenched, all-explaining racism of American society. The only one of these answers that it is permissible to voice in mainstream debate is the last.

The basic political aim of much multicultural scholarship is to explain away the lack of success of groups designated (in the case of blacks, with undeniable validity) as victims. However artful and diverting the phrasing, the purpose is to blame their failure on the people who have succeeded, turning that success from a legitimate source of pride into proof positive of blame. Underlying this effort is an unexamined assumption that talent is distributed absolutely evenly across lines of class, race, and gender and that differences in performance reflect only differences in opportunity, not differences in ability.

In truth, we don't know whether there are racial differences in intelligence because we don't want to find out. Research into the subject is taboo because, if it turns out that there are such differences, we have no means of handling the political implications. When I say the topic is taboo, I mean *really* taboo. A tenured professor at the University of Delaware was threatened with the loss of her job a few years ago for even considering taking a grant—to study entirely different matters related to heredity—from a foundation that had "tainted" itself by underwriting past research into racial differences.

The same willful ignorance is true in matters of gender. It is an axiom of the women's movement that ability of men and women is equal, not only in the aggregate but in all subcategories of intelligence (except, perhaps, for the ill-defined "women's intuition" that even many ardent feminists tend to claim as an asset for their sex). When men perform better on mathematical tests and women on verbal ones, this divergence is treated as proof per se of unequal socialization, not of anything inherent. That may well be right, but we don't know because our government is unwilling to fund massive, truly objective studies of the subject, and nearly all private research is colored by some political agenda.

Most of the past two decades of civil rights litigation have depended on the assumption that unequal results in the allocation of society's goodies automatically prove that the process for allotting them is unjust. If researchers demonstrated that racial or gender differences exist (I personally suspect they don't, but who really knows?), that rationale would obviously be invalidated. What would be the next step? To adjust the quotas downward by some debatable percentage? To throw them out altogether? To create some vast improvement scheme for minorities and women (or for white men, if it turns out they are the weaker performers)? Or perhaps, in keeping with the egalitarian spirit of our age, to declare that ability is not the prime criterion for employment anyway?

Without resolving whether racial prejudice is still holding blacks down or whether preference quotas are buoying them up—both are probably true, sometimes for the same individual—or whether any one person's talent is equal to his appointed task, we can say that a closer analysis of black economic experience suggests that the real problem has less to do with race than with the culture of poverty. In *Paved With Good Intentions: The Failure of Race Relations in Contemporary America,* Jared Taylor reports on economic research demonstrating that blacks and whites "who grew up under the same circumstances and went on to get similar educations show no difference in their average incomes." Among others, Taylor cites black scholar Walter Williams of George Mason University, who says that data about the comparable earnings of black and white women college graduates are "one of the best-kept secrets of all time and virtually totally ignored in the literature on racial differences." Taylor quotes Thomas Sowell, a black economist at the Hoover Institution, who says, "There is a positive hostility to analyses of black success if they suggest that racism may not be the cause of black failure." Taylor notes that while the black population doubled between 1950 and 1990, the number of black white-collar workers went up ninefold. He adds: "The number of blacks that are 'affluent' (earning more than $50,000 in inflation-adjusted dollars) went from one in seventeen in 1967 to one in seven in 1989." Of course many of these statistics reflect broader social trends in the United States; nonetheless, blacks were able to share in those improvements.

Troublingly, even as economic statistics demonstrate that things are getting better for black Americans, the black perception is that things are getting worse. In a May 1994 survey of more than a thousand blacks by Michael Dawson, a political science professor at the University of Chicago, some sixty-five percent said they did not expect racial equality to come within their lifetimes, and twenty-two percent say they did not expect it to come ever. Dawson found "a more radical black America than existed even five years ago," with burgeoning support for black nationalism or separatism. Sixty-two percent favored the creation of all-male public schools for blacks sixty-eight percent favored black control of government in majority-black areas, seventy-four percent called for black economic control in those areas, and eighty-one percent said blacks deserved a better chance legally, socially, and economically. Those sentiments were most pronounced among the young and poor, who appear to have given up hope of mainstream advancement.

At a deeper level, these blacks who do not participate in this economic rise may indeed be deemed victims of racism, for it surely played a major role in immersing them in the ghetto and poverty culture from which they find it so difficult to escape. But only historically is the underclass a product of racism; now it is the underclass primarily because it is culturally imprinted with the failings of the underclass.

The programs devised to deal with this grim reality generally do so by taking on the rather easier business of advancing privileged, middle-class blacks into the upper echelons of the mainstream. The most conspicuous have to do with college and graduate school admission, for which a dual standard exists virtually everywhere. Taylor reports that in most years, blacks who are admitted to medical school have lower average scores than whites who are rejected. The situation is almost as extreme in law schools. At the University of Texas, for example, white applicants generally need scores of approximately the ninety-second percentile on the nationally administered Law School Aptitude Test, while blacks scoring as low as the fifty-fifth percentile get in.

In the arts and sciences, the recruitment situation is especially dire. In 1986, Taylor notes, of some eight thousand doctorates awarded in the physical sciences and engineering, only thirty-nine went to blacks. Indeed, in that year there were only 820 doctorates awarded to blacks altogether. Half were in education, and there were none whatsoever in geology, aerospace engineering, astronomy, geometry, astrophysics, theoretical chemistry, European history, architecture, Russian, Spanish, German, or the classics. No wonder that so many academic departments fail to meet their affirmative action quotas.

The natural response to such troubling statistics is to redouble efforts to recruit black students into the top tier. But the Hoover Institution's Sowell says that may be self-defeating. Noting that two thirds of blacks at the University of California at Berkeley fail to graduate—including many who might have prospered at less competitive schools—Sowell urges that schools apply uniform admissions standards and let black students settle in at whatever level is comfortable. This would presumably increase their individual contentment and their collective rate of success. Says Sowell: "The issue is not whether minority students are 'qualified' to be in college, law schools, etc., but whether they are systematically mismatched with the particular institutions they are attending." A better match of circumstances would benefit not only them but white society as well. The best way to dispel assumptions of black inferiority is to observe black success firsthand. Watching an affirmative action beneficiary struggle to (not quite) keep up has the opposite effect.

In theory, as opposed to often ham-handed practice, affirmative action is not anti-elitist. It presupposes that blacks and whites are equally talented but unequally treated due to racism present and past. Its promoters even promise that on some future (and increasingly distant) day, the program will die away for lack of need. In truth, it is likely to die away whether or not blacks catch up in performance, because other racial and ethnic groups who do not share in white guilt are bound to be less and less willing to see blacks given a built-in advantage. Already blacks are less than half of the total minority population. Early in the next century, if it has not happened already, they will be bypassed by Hispanics as the largest single minority group. This is already true in cities such as Miami, Los Angeles, and New York, where the burgeoning Hispanic populations are demanding their proportional share. "It's the ultimate nightmare of affirmative action," says Ricky Gaull Silberman, vice chair of the federal Equal Employment Opportunities Commission, as quoted in a January 1994 report from the Newhouse News Service. "It is the Achilles' heel." Mamie Grant, who heads the organization representing black city workers in Los Angeles, protests about Hispanics: "They're trying to siphon off all our gains." Her counterpart in representing black workers countywide, Clyde Johnson, correctly says, "When you think of affirmative action, you think of black and white. All the laws were really directed specifically at eliminating patterns of discrimination against blacks." He adds with some bitterness, "All the others are latecomers and bandwagon jumpers." But as Latino activist Xavier Hermosilla of Los Angeles is quoted as saying, "They shall overcome. We shall *overwhelm.*"

For now, however, affirmative action is alive and well, and its operation is profoundly anti-elitist, not just against white candidates who lose out, but against the ablest blacks. The practical effect of affirmative action is to give places to mediocrities while causing white (and, for that matter, nonwhite) colleagues to view with suspicion the talents and credentials of all blacks newly given authority.

The drive for "a cabinet that looks like America" applies to almost every major corporation in America, not to mention universities and government offices. In my own business of journalism, I have lost count of the times I have heard senior executives of various media say that they have no openings but that there is a job available anytime for any adequately qualified black. This is not exactly a secret to the white staff. And it is not surprising that when black employees arrive, they face more than usual skepticism about whether they are really up to the job—which in turn makes them angry and mistrustful. Even among the best intentioned, affirmative action breeds racial resentment on both sides.

The blame for the inadequacies of affirmative action should be placed squarely on the shoulders of the white male executives who have had ultimate responsibility for administering these programs. Faced with the choice between the laborious and expensive process of locating, recruiting, and developing minority people of talent or the cheaper expedient of stealing them from somewhere else by overpaying them, many businesses have opted for the quick and dirty path. This means that the same few top-tier minority candidates—many of them of middle-class background and not conspicuously disadvantaged to begin with—keep rocketing up the career ladder, while the truly downtrodden get no great breaks. In other cases, companies treat minority hiring as just a part of overhead costs. They take on token employees to satisfy pressure groups and federal investigators but do not necessarily expect them to be able to perform, and frequently do not give them meaningful work to do. I remember being told by the chief executive of a large media corporation: "I've learned that you don't go out and find qualified blacks. You go out and you find blacks and you qualify them." There were two ways to interpret that statement: that companies must devote major resources to employee development, or that a shuck and jive to satisfy the quota checkers is sufficient. The executive seemed to believe his company was taking the former path, the high road. His employees, including many of the black ones, thought he was traveling the low road.

Quotas certainly have their place in redressing grievances. They make the most sense as a means of countering past officially sanctioned discrimination, such as in hiring for police and fire departments, admission to labor unions, and awarding of government contracts. They also make the most sense when the jobs involved fit the rationale for unions, i.e., the interchangeability of labor. In these situations, provided certain minimum standards are met, it makes little difference whether the person who ranks highest on a test gets a job. Does it really matter whether the cop on the beat has the best arithmetic skills of all candidates or whether the man on the fire truck is the best of all spellers? The tests are almost irrelevant; they are a sorting device.

Even in these circumstances, however, affirmative action quotas breed racial mistrust. They defy the rule-of-thumb elitism of everyday life. They suggest that the ostensibly equal fellow employee may in fact be a lot less swift, which can be a real problem in jobs where one's safety depends on the mental acuity of one's partners. And when the quotas operate by setting a lower passing score for one racial group—as opposed to having a common pool of the qualified but hiring underrepresented groups disproportionately often—the public may come to share doubts about the basic competence of their technicians, safety officers, and the like.

The real threat to elitism comes when affirmative action applies to jobs involving eight hours a day of brain work. For America to be at its most productive and competitive in a global economy, it should have the ablest possible talents occupying the key jobs. Even more, it should have a work force confident that meritocracy is the guiding principle in employment. Workers who believe that merit and merit alone will determine their fate are workers motivated to perform at their peak. The perception that quotas and favoritism, however benignly intentioned, are subverting the rule of merit turns employees resentful and imperils their productivity.

The most aggravating thing to many whites who see themselves as victims of reverse discrimination is the determination of the institutions that are showing favoritism to deny, or at least deflect, any suggestion that they are doing so. Cries of scandal and disgrace erupted at Georgetown Law School a couple of years ago when a student who had access to admissions and scholarship files made public the fact that black enrollees had had, over a period of several years, consistently lower average grades and standardized test scores than the whites admitted to the class. The outrage was directed at the young man who revealed this information, on the basis that he had violated a confidential trust. But the scorn should have been heaped on the institution for wishing to conceal information that concerned matters relevant to public policy—and that would certainly have been of interest to every white applicant who was turned down and, even more important, to every prospective employer of Georgetown Law graduates. A school that employs a double standard in admissions may well be employing a double standard in grading and certification, whether officially or de facto. If a black graduate of Georgetown Law does not necessarily embody the same level of competence as a white graduate of Georgetown Law, surely that is information that people relying on the reputation of Georgetown ought to have. And needless to say, it's not only Georgetown, and it's not only law school.

In truth, not very many sophisticated employers will be unaware of the double standard. They know full well that credentials of minority alumni may come with an invisible asterisk denoting the dual set of rules. So who is most apt to be victimized? Again, the minority candidate who could make it on a level playing field but whose accomplishments are initially, and perhaps always, suspect. That is the double bind of affirmative action. It begins with a presumption that all groups are equal, so their results in life should be equal. It then employs ameliorative mechanisms that end by enshrining the notion that the groups are not equal and probably never will be. As applied to the upper intellectual reaches of society, affirmative action is an idea that subverts its own aims.

Indeed, there is now a sizable body of thought, not all of it conservative or white, that questions the wisdom of continuing affirmative action unchanged. One of the most comprehensive challenges comes from the aforementioned Charles Murray of the American Enterprise Institute, writing in the May 22, 1992, issue of the *TLS.* In a review of Andrew Hacker's *Two Nations,* which he characterizes as a liberal apologia for everything from street crime to illegitimacy within the U.S. black community, Murray takes to task the section on affirmative action:

It is not easy to find excuses for Hacker this time. He is a college teacher. He knows—it is impossible that he does not know—how large differences in entrance test scores translate into performance in the classroom. He has to be aware of the white students' jokes about inadequately prepared black students, to have heard faculty members furtively discuss the double standards they have to use in grading blacks and whites, and to have observed a faculty recruiting process in which the standards for black candidates are not just a little easier, but worlds apart, from the standards for white male candidates. He has to be aware, in short, that affirmative action has led to a situation in America's universities where the median black student doesn't just have lower test scores, which can be brushed aside as cultural artefacts, and the median black professor doesn't just have fewer publications. Rather, they are conspicuously less competent than their median white counterparts at the same institution. It is this reality—not a figment of white youngsters' imagination, but their factually correct appraisal of the world they see around them, systematically fostered by affirmative action—that is shaping the attitudes of middle-class white youngsters about the abilities of blacks, and prompting much of the racial antagonism that Hacker laments.

Murray's bluntness struck a nerve in the distinguished black novelist Ishmael Reed, who wrote a letter of complaint containing an assertion that is increasingly popular among black men: "The chief beneficiaries of affirmative action are professional white women." Here is another of affirmative action's inherent contradictions. Blacks say the programs help other people more than them, yet cling to the quotas nonetheless as an all but eternal birthright engendered by the historical fact of slavery. Indeed, former Harvard Law School tenured professor Derrick Bell made the claim of eternal entitlement based on slavery in *Faces at the Bottom of the Well: The Permanence of Racism,* published in 1992. He labels slavery "an example of what white America has done [and] a constant reminder of what white America might do." He adds: "From the Emancipation Proclamation on, the Man has been handing us a bunch of bogus freedom checks he never intended to honor. . . . Americans achieve a measure of social stability through their unspoken pact to keep blacks at the bottom." This almost addictive attachment to past grievance was voiced from a less inflamed quarter in a November 1992 decision by a United States Court of Appeals in Cincinnati. The court ruled it was impermissible for a lower-level judge to dissolve a preferential hiring plan for minorities even after the original goal had been achieved. As reported in *The Washington Post,* the appeals court threw out a decision by a trial court to end a quota plan that had been in place in the Cincinnati municipal fire department for some eighteen years. When it was installed in 1974, the plan provided for separate white and minority hiring lists, with two jobs going to minorities for every three given to whites, regardless of test scores or total number of applicants. The goal was to get the share of minorities up to eighteen percent of the staff—a quota achieved by 1986. No matter. In 1992 the Appeals Court insisted the quota hiring remain in place because a secondary quota, having to do with promotions into higher jobs, had not yet been met. The promotion rate surely had something to do with the performance of minority applicants on the job and in civil service tests; advancement was within their grasp if they were good enough, especially in a department already committed to quotas. In any case, more forced minority hiring would do nothing directly to meet the additional quota. But the program could not end. Minorities were fixated on it, and would regard its end as a setback.

Just as irrational and compulsive was the continuation of the school desegregation order in Boston, which in 1974 had the valid purpose of undoing willful segregation by the elected school board. Long before it was lifted, however, so many whites had fled the school system that no amount of busing could achieve the original intention. There was no longer a white majority to be dispersed, and the whites who remained came from such straitened economic circumstances that they were not demonstrably better off than their black or Hispanic classmates. No longer relevant, the program survived by reflex for the better part of two decades.

No critic of affirmative action should forget the disgusting acts of the past that kept women and blacks out of jobs for which they were well qualified. As I was writing this chapter, Archie Williams died, fifty-eight years after his greatest triumph, winning the 1936 Olympic gold medal in the four-hundred-meter run. In later years, when Williams was asked how the racial supremacist Nazis had treated him, he would say, "Well, at least they didn't ask us to ride in the back of the bus." Williams was trained as an engineer. But no one was hiring black engineers, not even Olympic gold medalists, when he got out of school. So for a time his degree qualified him to dig ditches. He trained as a pilot, but no one was hiring black pilots. So he trained others in the military rather than have a lucrative commercial career. His story is tragically typical. Although its ending is happier, so is the saga of Sandra Day O'Connor. Although gifted enough to become the first woman Supreme Court justice, when she finished law school she couldn't even get interviews, let alone employment, at any substantial firm. Much the same happened to her new colleague Ruth Bader Ginsberg. Women were categorically ineligible, and that was that.

Understandably, many blacks and women fear that in the absence of affirmative action programs, those bad old days may recur. That is mistaking the means for the end. Affirmative action programs came about because of social progress in attitudes toward blacks and women. The schemes were judicially or legislatively mandated, or voluntarily adopted, *because* the general public viewed social change and perhaps redress as a good thing. A farewell to particular schemes would not in itself roll back commitment to social progress any more than their survival makes social progress popular. In fact, a farewell to quotas might engender great goodwill among whites and, for that matter, self-esteem among blacks for daring to brave unregulated, meritocratic competition.

This same social progress may have made it possible for us to face the possibility—not, in my view, a probability, but possible enough—that there may be inherent racial differences in potential and performance. We will probably never determine to everyone's satisfaction if that is so. For one thing, the research will likely remain taboo. This is one area where the First Amendment does not run. And if the research were undertaken, it would be almost impossible to screen for social variables and get truly comparable groups. In fact, the case is often made that it can never be truly comparable to be black or to be white in American society, that the mere fact of race and how it is perceived overshadows everything else. Last and not least, assertions about racial difference rest on erroneous assumptions of racial purity. Instead, the vast majority of American "blacks" probably have some white, Indian, or Hispanic ancestry, and many whites from "old" families are apt to have unacknowledged black or Indian forebears. So it would be very difficult to validate test groups of sufficient whiteness or blackness; and once they were studied, findings about them would not apply with any clarity to the large portions of the population that are racially mixed. But set the concept of testing aside and allow, in anecdotal or vernacular discussion, for the possibility of difference. Perhaps it would mean that, in a society sans affirmative action, somewhat fewer blacks than whites would go to college, fewer would become lawyers or doctors, fewer would run large corporations. Would it matter? Arguably not, as long as everyone who is qualified has a chance and more than a few minority candidates actually continue to make it. America's doors will never again be closed to blacks. Perhaps it is time to stop thinking of blacks—and having them think of themselves—as a category. Let them rise or fall as individuals. That would be, in the moral and metaphysical sense, an affirmative action. The measure of a just society is not whether a demographically proportional share of any group succeeds, but whether any individual of talent can succeed regardless of what group he belongs to. If all groups seek to belong to an elite, let us have an elite based once again on elitism.

The second great multicultural threat to elitism, the notion of the interchangeability or at least comparability of cultures, has roots closely related to affirmative action. Quotas are meant to guide blacks to equality in the present. Multicultural theory is meant to give them a sense of equality about their past. This is often a flight from reality, no more valid for being wholly understandable. If Africa was indeed the womb of civilization, as many Afrocentric scholars assert, it certainly has not been so for a thousand years, maybe twice that long. And when it was a true world power, in the heyday of pharaonic Egypt, the peak creativity arose in a civilization far removed in place as well as time from the ancestral lands of most American blacks. It is unlikely that Egyptians did, as many Afrocentrists claim, master glided flight or invent electrical batteries and electroplating or discover the principles of quantum mechanics, Darwinian evolution, gravity, and the wave-particle duality of light. Even if they did, how does that ennoble sub-Saharan black Africans? They were not Egyptian rulers. They were subjugated people, in the United States, in Latin America, in the Caribbean, in Europe. Even more painfully for blacks who see Islam as their appropriate religion, Africans were a subjugated people in Arabia. Some Africans were trapped by slavers because they were not quick enough or cunning enough to get away. Some were sold into slavery by fellow blacks, either marauding native tribes or on occasion their own kinsmen. Slavery was a moral blot on its white perpetrators. It was a blot on many black tribes as well.

As for African cultural achievements, they are real enough. Anyone who has visited the splendid (if ill-maintained) African art collection in the museum in Dakar, capital of Senegal, or surveyed the Benin bronzes at the Smithsonian in Washington can perceive the beauty, craftsmanship, and sophistication of African art. Like most great art of the past, it found its inspiration in religion, which is natural enough—religion, like art, is based on metaphor. The great pyramids of ancient Zimbabwe bespeak both an esthetic vision and an ambitious and enduring empire. The long and arduous trade routes of ancient Africans, along trails that daunted Burton, Livingstone, and other European explorers, are evidence of social organization and economic awareness. In politics and warfare, tales of empire abound. The Zulus were sufficiently disciplined and shrewd to fight English forces in South Africa to a virtual standstill.

New scholarly evidence emerges all the time of African heritage. The past few years have brought a succession of museum exhibits and permanent installations celebrating the civilization that flourished just to the south of Egypt—in Nubia, the world's first black nation. A cultural and military power that supplied gold, slaves, and exotic animals to the Mediterranean nations, Nubia was, by turns, Egypt's rival, its trading partner, its vassal state, and its conqueror. Nubian pharaohs reigned over a prosperous, united North African empire from 715 B.C. to 656 B.C.

Drawing on three decades of excavations and study, these exhibitions have revealed Nubia as Egypt's virtual equal rather than its subordinate. "In the classical period, the Nubians were treated with tremendous respect. They were viewed as some of the most successful warriors," says Emily Teeter, assistant curator at the Oriental Institute Museum in Chicago. She was one of a number of scholars interviewed by my *Time* colleague, art historian Daniel Levy, from whom I gratefully gleaned this passage. According to Daniel, Herodotus and other ancient Greeks told many tales honoring the strength, wealth, and beauty of the Nubian kingdom of Kush. Some historians believe the concept of kingship originated in Nubia, as did the notion, borrowed by Egypt, that a secular king is an earthly god. Yet the civilization's monumental ruins, gold jewelry, burnished pottery, and animated statuary have long been hidden in the sands, damaged by looters and unreachable because of war, famine, and inaccessible roads.

Much of ancient Nubia vanished when Egypt opened the Aswan High Dam in the 1960s. That event prompted an international effort to study known sites before they were submerged below 1,930 square miles of water from the newly created Lake Nasser. Thirty archaeological teams from twenty-five countries saved numerous temples and tombs, such as Abu Simbel, the rock-hewn Egyptian temple of Ramses II, which was reconstructed on higher ground far from the water's way. Excavators uncovered tens of thousands of vessels, jewels, and statuary, which they sent to museum laboratories for scholars and scientists to study, catalogue, clean, and reconstruct. As is usual with scholars, it has taken decades.

Nubian artwork reflects, ironically, a true melting pot of disparate artistic influences. Excavations are continuing, and scholars still have thousands of objects to study and much to learn about this once-great civilization. One mystery is Meroitic, the Nubian language, which remains only partly deciphered. Other intriguing questions surround the extent of Nubia's influence on Rome and Greece, as well as on the evolution of Africa.

All this is of value to anyone interested in the making of the modern world. So are more contemporary studies of tribal political organization, trade routes, nomadic ecology, and the subtleties of rhythm structure in African music. Indeed, in a perverse way there is something to be gained in studying why so many African women willingly, even eagerly, continue to submit their daughters to the horrific mutilation of the clitoris and vulva euphemized as "female circumcision." Without joining the appalling number of Afrocentrist scholars who try to defend this as indigenous tradition, one can recognize that here is a way of coming to grips with a truly alien world.

But that does not mean that studying African culture is any kind of substitute for studying Euro-American culture, even for American children of African descent. Indeed, in a comprehensive trashing of Afrocentrism in the *TLS* in February 1993, Professor Kwame Anthony Appiah of Harvard's Afro-American studies department begins by challenging the very notion that there is such a thing as "African culture" in the singular rather than the plural. "It is surely preposterous," he writes, "to suppose that there is a single African culture, shared by everyone from the civilizations of the Upper Nile thousands of years ago to the thousand or so language-zones of contemporary Africa. In aiming to identify some common core of African civilization, the Afrocentrists seem once again to be responding to earlier attempts to identify a common core of Western culture. One can be forgiven for wondering just how unitary the West really is today. But it was always a strange idea that Alexander, Alfred and Frederick the Great[s] had something in common with each other and with the least of their subjects, which could be called Western culture. And in Africa, where whatever continuity there has been through all this time has not been mediated by even the broken textual tradition that in some sense unites 'Western culture,' it is not only a strange idea but a silly one." Appiah is alert to such solecisms as the popular use of Swahili words to teach ostensibly African virtues in the ceremonies of Kwanzaa, the "black Christmas" now observed by an estimated ten million Americans. "There is something of an irony in the use of Swahili as an Afrocentric language, since hardly any of the slaves brought to the New World can have known it, and it was in fact being used in a culture in which slave-trading to the Arabian peninsula was a major element of the economy." He devastatingly demonstrates how supposedly Afrocentric scholars lack knowledge of historical Africa. For instance, he asserts that the foremost American figure in Afrocentrism, the much-quoted and consistently vitriolic Molefi Assante of Temple University, "has written whole books about Akan culture without referring to the major works of such Akan philosophers as J. B. Danquah, William Abrahams, Kwasi Wiredu, and Kwame Gyekye." Appiah adds: "I am reliably informed that, on one occasion not so long ago, a distinguished Zairian intellectual was told by an African-American interlocutor that 'We do not need you educated Africans coming here to tell us about African culture.' "

Appiah, whose black father was one of the founders of independent Ghana and whose white mother was the daughter of Sir Stafford Cripps, Chancellor of the Exchequer in a British Labor cabinet, is an astute scholar of modern Africa and a respectful listener to philosophical constructs that are truly non-European. But he dismisses most American versions of Afrocentrism as "Eurocentrism upside down." He is particularly tough on the claim articulated in such books as Clinton M. Jean's *Behind the Eurocentric Veils*—which Appiah nonetheless describes as among the best Afrocentric books he has read —that "African culture (is) centrally more humane than Western culture."

This claim crops up time and again in Afrocentric "scholarship." It is central to the teachings (one cannot say writings, because there do not seem to be any of substance) of the laughable Leonard Jeffries, who came to national prominence for his anti-Semitic ravings and his categorical denunciations of whites as "ice people" during his two-decade-plus tenure as chairman of black studies at City College of New York. Jeffries, who won a $400,000 damage judgment by asserting that his chairmanship was stripped in 1992 in response to his exercise of free speech, has an official departmental policy of favoring conferences and panels over research. That may be connected to the fact, unearthed by fellow professors who searched the archives, that Jeffries has apparently done no research of his own. He does, however, propound theories, of which his most publicized is the claim that the skin pigment melanin gives blacks intellectual superiority, while their status as "sun people" also makes them warmer, kinder, and more communal. This "melanist" theory, of which Jeffries is, alas, not the only proponent, has rapidly become pervasive among black professors. They organize conferences, attended by exceptionally gullible holders of doctorates, to amplify a misreading of a speculative scientific paper published in 1983 by San Francisco surgeon Frank Barr about the significance of neuromelanin. This substance is markedly different from the skin pigment of which blacks do indeed have a larger supply; in fact, neuromelanin is present in similar amounts in all human beings of whatever race. Nonetheless, melanists attribute to neuromelanin the abilities to convert light and magnetic fields to sound, to be a superconductor, and to capture sunlight and hold it in "memory mode"; some of them describe melanin granules as minicomputers that can respond and analyze without interacting with the brain. All of them say melanin makes blacks inherently superior. Says Barr, "I wrote a paper for a theoretical journal about specific properties of an interesting, neglected molecule. It included no stupid things like the more melanin you have, the smarter you are." But the adherents to melanism are untroubled by Barr's alarm. Dr. Patricia Newton, a psychiatrist at Johns Hopkins University, enthused about melanin at the black National Medical Association convention in 1993. She claimed that melanin, "one of the strongest electromagnetic field forces in the universe," had the capacity to make blacks intellectually better than other races and also was a stimulus to dance. "It's your melanin that makes you do it. When you hear that bass drum, it creates a melatonin increase surge, causing it to be released in the body, inducing opiates of the endorphin and enkephalin systems, and gives you a sense of well-being." The down side, she added, is that melanin makes blacks genetically more susceptible to narcotic addiction.

There are dissenters. John Warfield, who headed the African American Studies Center at the University of Texas at Austin, calls melanism "a difficult concept to support scientifically" and "a response reflective of some of the destitution in the black community." In any case, this bad science would not much matter if its promulgation were confined to those old enough to know better. But many of those duped by melanism are too young to spot its illogic.

Gladys Twyman, coordinator of the African American Infusion Program for Atlanta public schools, says, "We have ten organizing principles on which our curriculum is based. The thread, the core of the project, is the concept of melanin."

The melanist emphasis on the "communal" virtues of

blacks—a merit commonly attributed by pseudo-scholarly advocates to such other complainant groups as women, Hispanics, and Indians—is an enticingly phrased assault on the elitist values of individualism and achievement. "Communal" people do not, of course, seek to outstrip each other or amass individual fortunes. They share things and support each other. This celebration of communality is steeped in the still-fashionable Marxism of academe and in the pervasive, perfervid desire to discredit competitions that the communal groups fear they may not be able to win. This colloquy reveals a deep contradiction similar to that engendered by affirmative action. On the one hand, proponents assert that cultures are not better or worse than one another, just different. Yet the special pleaders cannot resist sneaking in moral or sentimental argument that some cultures are indeed better—and that on humanitarian grounds, non-European cultures can make that claim.

It is, of course, the assertion of superiority for African culture that gives Afrocentrism its political appeal in contemporary America. The underlying notion is that black children need pride in their identity if they are to learn and succeed. Mainstream schools are failing dismally in many black neighborhoods now, so officials who know better have been persuaded to try this academic slumgullion of, as Appiah phrases it, "truth and error, insight and illusion, moral generosity and meanness." One problem is that the curriculum tends to be laxly supervised, both because its intent is political as much as pedagogic and because many Afrocentric teachers reject normal standards of proof and rationality as just more hateful Eurocentrism. Thus black children are taught—or at least come away believing—that blacks invented the telephone, the elevator, the light bulb, and a great many other things that racist whites refuse to credit them for. In truth blacks made significant contributions to the development of much modern technology, and their role, or indeed the presence of an educated black class of the nineteenth and early twentieth century, does tend to be downplayed. But blacks did not "invent" all these technological advances, and it cannot do much for the future cause of race relations to have a whole generation of blacks growing up in the erroneous belief that they did. When whites disagree, their argument will likely be viewed as a racist assault rather than the truth.

When it comes to American history, elementary school ought to teach children perspective and forgiveness about the sins of the past. Instead, today's classroom often seems to teach them to hold figures of the past personally and morally responsible for the prevailing ethos of their times. In June 1993 national media reported on the reopening of Teddy Roosevelt's Sagamore Hill, which had been renovated with funds that schoolchildren had a hand in allocating. One of the reasons they favored Roosevelt's home over George Washington's Shadow Lawn, it was explained, is that Roosevelt did not own slaves. Apparently no teacher had conveyed to these junior makers of moral distinctions the significance of one man's having been born in 1732 and the other in 1858. It is typical of the hostile, aggrieved posture of multiculturalists to discredit men who were virtuous by the mores of their times through the retroactive imposition of today's values and beliefs.

At a deeper level, what is wrong with Afrocentrism is the assumption that American children of black descent owe more to African culture than to European. This is nonsense. If anything, black Americans, whose ancestors have been here for centuries in most cases, are more deeply rooted in American culture and values than many more recent émigrés, even from Europe. And American institutions are not, except on the margins, derived from African ones. European culture is not alien to black Americans. Even as radical a figure as W.E.B. Du Bois said, "I do not wince when I read Shakespeare." He was prepared, as disappointingly few multiculturalists are today, to acknowledge the existence of universal values and insights, ideas transcending their place and time. But many contemporary black scholars labor to assert African origins for much of what they admire in black American history. For example, Johnnetta Cole, president of Spelman College in Atlanta and an early candidate for a Clinton cabinet post, has argued that the black insurance companies that built early Atlanta fortunes derived less from European capitalism than from quasi-socialist mutual self-help organizations found in African communities. There may indeed be points worthy of comparison to African models. But the founding businessmen (one of whom modeled his still-standing home on the architectural features he liked in European palaces) and their customers were surely aware that they were emulating the white insurance business. In truth, this probably helped make the concept more, rather than less, credible within the black community.

An even more labored attempt to de-Europeanize an obviously European institution is made in the March/April 1993 issue of *The Black Collegian,* in which writer Linda Bates Parker tries to equate college commencement with "rites of passage ceremonies and rituals [that] date back to the earliest known traditions of man, which have their roots in Africa." By that genealogy, *everything* has its roots in Africa. But then, isn't that supposed to be the point?

No reasonable person can argue that African culture was materially superior to European; the reasons range from enslavement to illiteracy. But that does not make Americans of African descent inferior to Americans of European or any other descent. The error is in looking for a group basis, a categorical basis, for pride. One's worth and self-regard ought to come from individual competitive performance, not from group identity. Pride based on clan or tribal connections is atavistic. It appeals to people who fear they cannot succeed as individuals, and by diverting their energies it all but ensures that they *will* not succeed as individuals.

One of the most troublesome aspects of reaction against "Eurocentrism" is the surprisingly prevalent view that reason and science are not absolute goods but mere cultural choices, no better or worse than other, more intuitive ways of "knowing." Reason and science are indeed hallmarks of Western civilization. They are the two biggest reasons for its superiority and worldwide dispersion. Probably some readers are wondering whether my antirationalist target is a chimera, a phantasm conjured by a fevered brain. Let me quote, without prefatory comment, an all too typical example from a *TLS* review of Christopher Jencks's liberal and compassionate book *Rethinking Social Policy: Race, Poverty and the Underclass:* "Jencks moves, armed with facts, with values which he takes care to expound, and a great trust in Enlightenment rationality. *Rethinking Social Policy* is an important book for these reasons. It is also for these reasons that critics will find limitations in it—by invoking other values, other facts and other, nonrationalistic forms of knowledge. While invoking such alternatives may always have been possible, it is particularly possible today, when a multiplicity of critical voices and forms of knowledge are increasingly gaining at least a minimum of recognition." What kind of world do we live in when "nonrationalistic" assertions can be considered a plausible response? When racial self-assertion and invective à la Jeffries can be part of a "multiplicity of critical voices" to be heeded? When it is viewed as progress that the irrational has more of a place at the table of serious debate? This salute to unreason is the reductio ad absurdum of multiculturalism, which in its elemental state is recognizable to anyone who ever spent time around a schoolyard ball game: If one can't win, then one changes the rules.

Of all the ways in which multiculturalism pretends that minority children do not need a traditional education—indeed, that they can better protect their integrity and identity without one—the cruelest is the crusade against linguistic assimilation. Standard English is, will continue to be, and in the majority opinion *should* be the essential minimum for participation in the economic, political, and cultural life of America. Fluency in other languages or dialects is admirable, and more Americans ought to make themselves multilingual. What passes for polylinguistic excellence in this country would seem barely sufficient to a Swiss chambermaid. But English is the American language, and court decisions notwithstanding, real facility in English should be required for naturalization, a driver's license, working papers, and, above all, the right to vote. Instead, we have teachers who argue, ostensibly with their students' interests at heart, that schools should teach black English so that pupils can hear in the classroom the authentic language of their streets. And we have cities such as Miami, where it is possible to be a nominally transitional bilingual student from kindergarten right through the senior year of high school without ever taking a schedule of classes taught entirely in English.

Even if black English does have the grammatical and syntactical rules that its proponents say give it the status of a dialect, it is not the dialect spoken in the world of American business, industry, and government. It is a dialect that instantly brands the speaker as part of an isolated minority, and by its resemblance to a degenerate, subliterate version of mainstream language it suggests that the speaker is ignorant or stupid.

The issue is a little more complicated when it involves the (mostly black) immigrants from Caribbean islands where Creole, pidgin, or some other English-derived patois is spoken. Language scholars say that Caribbean speech, which varies from island to island, is a truly new language, blending elements of ancestral West African languages with bits from the colonial tongues of English, Spanish, French, and Dutch. But the speakers by and large think of their patois as English, and they are sensitive to suggestions that they are speaking something else. Equally, they are sensitive to suggestions that their version of English is substandard or deviant. Elizabeth Coelho, author of *Caribbean Students in Canadian Schools,* was quoted in the November 28, 1992, *New York Times* as saying that the label of "broken English" implies that Creole is deficient. "If you think of your language as deficient," she added, "then how do you think of yourself?" Her tenderness is admirable, but this sort of coddling from reality is likely to keep students from bettering themselves and then resolving to better the social conditions and educational performance in their home-lands—which are, by economic and hygienic standards, frequently deficient indeed.

The most nettlesome issues of linguistic assimilation concern native speakers of Spanish, who now number about eighteen million American residents, according to the 1990 United States census. They are the largest of a sizable and growing group of Americans who now speak something other than English at home. Some 31.8 million Americans, or one in seven, greet the day in some other tongue than English. That number is up by a third in just ten years since the previous census. The number of Spanish speakers is up by more than fifty percent, accounting for the overwhelming majority of the change. (The only other native language spoken by more than a million Americans that increased significantly is Chinese, whose speakers doubled in a decade to about 1.25 million.) Not all these preservers of ancestral tongues are inadequate in English by any means. One of those who celebrate this linguistic diversity is the articulate Ling-Chi Wang, a 1966 immigrant to San Francisco who is now chairman of the Asian ethnic studies department at the University of California at Berkeley. He told the Associated Press in 1993 that he regarded the proliferation of languages as a national asset. "What unfortunately has happened in the past," he said, "is that we do our very best to wipe out whatever linguistic abilities our children have and then spend millions in colleges across the country trying to re-teach these students foreign languages." To Wang, multilingualism is a political and economic benefit to America in a global economy: "We live in a world that is shrinking rapidly. It is no longer what it was in the nineteenth century, when it was dominated by European colonial powers."

If multilingualism were operating as Wang so happily fantasizes, there would be no thriving English-only movement. If people limited their use of other languages to home, for sentimental reasons, and to international commerce, and honored English in the street, the demographic changes overtaking America would alarm many fewer European-descent whites. In truth, the goal of many Hispanic advocates is to create inclusive subcultures in which it will not be necessary to take up English to participate in any aspect of community life. In May 1993 the Dade County commission, representing metropolitan Miami, repealed an "English only" ordinance requiring that the county's official business be done in English. This repealed rule did not affect private transactions at all, except if they had to be recorded in public documents. Exceptions to the English-only rule were already in place for matters involving emergency and safety issues and for voting. Osvaldo Soto, president of the triumphant Spanish American League Against Discrimination, said by way of certifying the need for the change: "Miami is now in reality the capital of the Americas. It doesn't make sense to have an anti-bilingual ordinance." *The capital of the Americas.* What does that mean, if not an open assertion that the Spanish speakers of Miami seek to orient themselves more toward Hispanic residents of other countries than toward the English speakers in the northern United States? Miguel Diaz de la Portilla, a county commissioner and the son of Cuban immigrants, asked rhetorically, "What is the American culture? Who's going to define it? We're a country of immigrants." Defining American culture is a lot easier if the definitions are written in one common language, English. And while this may be a nation of immigrants, every prior generation of them accepted the practical necessity of that common tongue.

Florida and California have passed state constitutional amendments declaring English the official language. But legislators fearful of Hispanic voting strength have declined to pass enabling laws, so the amendments remain largely symbolic. Arizona voters passed a law designating English as the official language in 1988, but it has been declared unconstitutional by a federal judge, and appeals were pending at the time this chapter was written. A measure of the defiant mood among Hispanics there was the appalling decision by Federal District Court Judge Aldredo Marquez in June 1993 to hold a citizenship swearing-in ceremony primarily in Spanish. (The actual oath would be administered in English, he said through a spokesman from the Tucson office of the Immigration and Naturalization Service.) The judge said that the ceremony would be more meaningful if conducted in the participants' native tongue. The "meaning," to this writer at least, was that they would not have to give up that tongue in any way in order to be good Americans—a legally accurate message, perhaps, but an unhealthy one. Interestingly, no law bars conducting the citizenship ceremony in a language other than English, presumably because it never occurred to Congress that any sitting judge would be so contemptuous of national unity. Said P. George Tryfiates, executive director of the Virginia-based English First, "This is multiculturalism run amok." Actually, it is worse than that. It is a glimpse into a troubling future.

A great many of my compassionate liberal friends share my horror at the divisive prospects of a multilinguistic society but believe that one aspect, bilingual school classes, are a necessary kindness to new arrivals. I'm not so sure. For a cover essay on bilingualism in *Time* a few years ago, I read more than a dozen books of educational research, from which I concluded that the one dependable way to enhance immigrants' facility in

English is to immerse them in it from the first possible moment. Bilingualism appeared to be helpful in some studies, but it impeded pupils' progress in others. The biggest proponents of bilingualism are those adult community leaders whose careers, in politics or social service or whatever, depend on preserving Hispanic group identity rather than promoting individual achievement. This may serve their narrow interests, but does it serve their constituents' interests, or society's?

It is possible to be elitist and competitive within a Spanish-speaking enclave, of course. Spanish-speaking countries produce plenty of capable doctors, lawyers, professors, and the like. But can linguistically separate sectors of society adequately appreciate each other's attainments? And if elitism takes place in the context of an orientation toward Cuba or Mexico or Latin America in general, does it have value and relevance for the United States economy and culture? Perhaps it will promote international business and understanding. Perhaps it will demystify the dreaded Yanqui. Perhaps instead it will simply siphon talent out of mainstream institutions and promote division.

Today it is street signs in Spanish or Chinese or Korean. Will tomorrow, when the Hispanic share of the nation is even larger, bring calls for self-governance, for a designated portion of the federal budget, for quasi-autonomous regions in the fashion of a southerly Québec? That vision of the future is a logical extension of present trends, and it is implicit in any assertion that the definition of America is up for grabs. America has faced immigrants before who wanted to be in, but not *of,* the new land. Three things make today different. First, the sheer numbers of Hispanics. Second, their linguistic bond and their proximity to other countries that share it. Third, the ideology of multiculturalism, which validates their separatism and brands would-be integrationists as racists.

It may seem a bit off target to blame multiculturalism, with its pretensions to scholarly innovation, for the last two items on my list of its affronts to elitism—the sanctioning of drugs, crime, and other social ills of urban youth and the pervasive notion among young blacks that speaking well and studying hard are "acting white." Both of these outlooks are, however, closely connected to the underlying tenet of all multiculturalism, to wit, that people who are not white and of northwestern European descent are fundamentally different. By this reasoning, the minorities labeled multicultural think differently, behave differently, subscribe to different values and standards, seek different goals, and neither can nor should be held to norms of white conduct. It may seem compassionate to say that drugs and crime and dropping out of school are a predictable, comprehensible response to the life of the urban underclass. But embracing these horrors, however common, as legitimate norms goes much further toward validating despair than any amount of poverty or even, perhaps, official racism. An elitist society expects people to make the most of themselves, and a surprising number do. A multicultural society seemingly conveys to its young that any identity is valid, provided that it is embraced with sufficient enthusiasm. Among young blacks, multiculturalism seems to go even deeper into destruction, suggesting that there is something truly alien in all achievement, that class and race solidarity requires that all blacks remain mired in defiant ignorance.

For evidence that the tacit sanctioning of youth crime and drug use is going on, I can only refer you to any major newspaper. Liberal tolerance gone haywire can be found in nearly every story on the subject. The pernicious particularity of the "acting white" charge was brought to my attention by my *Time* colleagues Sophronia Scott and David Thigpen, who found credible instances nationwide of young black people who had been scorned, assaulted, even threatened with death for the racial crime of getting good grades and wanting to go to college. Envy among the lower orders (or the higher ones) is nothing new in human history. But multiculturalist theory and schooling give a spurious legitimacy, a kind of tribal validation, to adolescent resentments.

Here is a sad irony. The big black hero among whites in recent years was the late Arthur Ashe, a man who never forgot his ethnicity (he said being black was a bigger burden than his two heart attacks or his fatal infection with AIDS) but who, equally, never let it stand in the way of wide-ranging intellectual achievement. Among blacks, especially black youth, the biggest black hero of the last couple of years was the late Malcolm X, less for the inner peace he eventually achieved than for the fiery way that he "dissed" whites. Michael Jordan's reckless gambling and the cock-of-the-walk promiscuity of Wilt Chamberlain and Magic Johnson do not seem to have diminished their popularity within the African American community. Maybe their dissolute behavior is defined as "acting black." If so, it is a definition worthy of the National Socialist White People's Party, not of blacks themselves.

Perhaps it is unfair to blame on multicultural scholars a range of behavior that some of them would likely discourage. Their aim, after all, is to call attention to black achievements, real or asserted. Some of them doubtless feel they are promoting a kind of elitism, too, albeit in a different context. Yet when all is said and done, the answer to black, Hispanic, or any other sense of exclusion from the mainstream must be to bolster boldness and self-confidence, not to concoct alternative scholarship or install alternative institutions. America has many races. It needs only one culture, the more inclusive the better.

FOUR

Why Can't a Man
Be More Like a Woman?

"Woman: the female of man. See *Homo.*"
—Complete Encyclopædia Britannica entry for *woman,*
first edition, 1771

WHENEVER the feminist movement gets a bit captious or silly—as in the 1993 fuss over whether there were enough statues of women in public parks and plazas in New York City—it is surely useful to remind oneself that many women, especially the best educated and most historically aware among them, are ablaze with rage over the way things used to be. To be born female was, by and large, to be born with limited horizons and few options. That was true not only in the eighteenth century and the ones that preceded it, but in the nineteenth and indeed the twentieth. I have seen the warping effects of frustration in the mothers of my friends; these women married and gave birth to successful men but found no place in the public world themselves, and their dammed-up drive often went into oversteering the careers of their husbands and children. My own mother regretted all her adult life that she had majored in English rather than her true love, physics, because she had been convinced by older women (including her aunt, a pioneer college dean) that the sciences were not "ladylike." Katharine Graham, perhaps the most powerful woman in America, has observed, "Power is neither male nor female." But Graham came to power the way almost every woman in history got there, up to virtually the present moment: through inheritance and marriage. Power may be neutral, but the road to it has been signposted by gender.

Having said all that, a dispassionate observer must still find it curious that women, a literal majority of the American population and holders of a large majority of its private wealth, have managed to get themselves classified as a minority group. They continue to enjoy advantages in recruitment and promotion long after the doors once closed to them have been flung wide open. It may still be hard for a woman to become a firefighter or steelworker; taunting or outright harassment of those who do crash the barrier is frequent and disgraceful (although reflective, for good or ill, of how male locker room louts also treat each other). In terms of jobs that matter in the formation of thought and allocation of resources, however—in other words, jobs for the elite—the evidence proving access for women is incontrovertible. Barely a quarter of a century after the women's movement began to make its mark, a third or more of all medical school, law school, and business school graduates are women, according to Census Bureau figures published in *The Washington Post.* By the same count, forty-six percent of the nation's financial managers are women, and so are forty-two percent of biologists and thirty-nine percent of mathematics professors—to name just three fields considered resistant to women and in which women traditionally were thought not to excel. In psychology, public relations, and my own niche of journalism, women now appear to be an absolute majority. While women still feel underrepresented in elective government (in part because they will not vote as a block for a fellow female in anything like the same percentages that, say, blacks will give to a fellow black), the gender ratio in the managerial ranks of the civil service is nearly fifty-fifty. Few women run major corporations, but many in the middle management generation seem to be well on their way.

Quotas, by whatever euphemism they are known, have become superfluous. Their primary effect, as with blacks, is to de-credential candidates who could have succeeded without help. Whenever quotas are operating, a woman who gets a good job is apt to be viewed as having arrived there solely because she is a woman—and in her heart of hearts is apt to ask herself if that might really be true.

The moral rationale for affirmative action on behalf of women is even weaker than the political and economic one. When blacks point to the cumulative effects of slavery and racial discrimination as a basis for giving them special advantages, they are speaking as an identifiable community. Both they themselves and the larger society around them have viewed them as a collective entity. In every generation up to the present one, and to a distressing extent even today, blacks have been born into families apt to be disadvantaged socially, educationally, and economically, have grown up in neighborhoods where similar disadvantages were the norm, and have entered schools and workplaces prone to perceive them as automatically inferior. It does not take much imagination to trace a clear hereditary line from the injustices of the past to the inadequacies of the present. Even so, the time must come when affirmative action gives way to open competition. As suggested in the previous chapter, when it comes to elite jobs, that time is already here.

Women, by contrast, can claim no such hereditary burden. Their sense of historical grievance is largely irrelevant and almost entirely self-imposed. Whatever happened to women in the past, it is only minimally visited upon women of today. Feminist anger is primarily a theoretical and ideological, not a practical, construct. Novelist Michael Crichton summed up the absurdity of much such posturing by privileged women in his latest socially astute best seller *Disclosure*. A careworn husband whose wife starts running a feminist guilt trip on him says in reply, "You're a partner in a law firm, for Christ's sake. You're about as oppressed as Leona Helmsley."

Yes, women are descended from a long line of thwarted women. They are equally descended from a long line of admittedly unthwarted men. The spiritual connection with female forebears may seem stronger, but the biological link is exactly the same. The distribution of children by gender remains roughly fifty-fifty no matter the social class of the parents, so women cannot claim, as blacks can, to have been born into comparative economic privation.

It is true that adult women tend to be paid less than men and to be grouped disproportionately on the lower rungs of the economic ladder. Susan Faludi's *Backlash* and its ideological kin notwithstanding, that variance is attributable to many other factors besides overt prejudice. Women are often less educated or credentialed. They tend to be employed in fields that society rewards less extravagantly (some women, ill versed in the workings of the free market or temperamentally inclined to the folly of Marxism, see that fact of life as some sort of conspiracy). In no-nonsense economic terms, women tend to be less committed to their careers. They take time away to have children. They are ready to stay home or leave work abruptly when one of those children is sick or when an aging parent is in trouble. They often object on family grounds to long and irregular hours or abruptly scheduled travel and other normal, male-accepted demands of a job. All these outside concerns are socially valid, but they get in the way of work. Many women who also see themselves as caregivers want the rules of the workplace rewritten to suit their personal needs. Indeed, they want their relative lack of commitment (or, as they would phrase it, alternative set of priorities) treated as something admirable and reward-worthy in a business setting. That attitude almost never wins appreciation from an employer and has rarely if ever led men to success; still, women argue that past and proven ways of doing business are irredeemably commingled with "sexism." In personal style, moreover, women tend to be less aggressive and confrontational than men while performing in an economy that seeks and compensates those go-getter qualities.

The real goal of many in the women's movement, I have come to feel, is not to change the way women think about themselves—breaking psychological fetters so they can maximize their potential—but to change the way men think, both about women and about themselves. This is nakedly true in matters of sex and its accompaniments, from workplace flirtation to pornography. For such ideologues as Catharine MacKinnon and Andrea Dworkin, it is not enough to civilize men's public behavior. They want to eradicate men's most private fantasies. If men titillate themselves with visions of rape, bondage, and domination, if they respond erotically to the idea of women as submissive (I guess I'd better add here that I don't), it does not mean that they are all going to turn into Ted Bundy—or even Clarence Thomas. Fantasies are just that, fantasies. They often serve as a therapeutic outlet, and in most lives they have nothing to do with actual or contemplated behavior. Some feminists and a great many Christian fundamentalists contend that fantasies inevitably lead to deeds, and cite such aberrant creatures as Bundy to prove the point. Given the relative handful of serial killers and the tens of millions of people who at least sample pornography, the causal link is, to put it mildly, flimsy. Some "scholars" go even further. In *Lewd Women & Wicked Witches: A Dynamics of Male Domination,* Marianne Hester of Britain's Exeter University asserts, "Heterosexual sex which women consent to is in actual fact a part of women's oppression." Hester's thinking was presumably influenced by Britain's Leeds Revolutionary Feminist Group, which in 1979 determined that "it is specifically through sexuality that the fundamental oppression, that of men over women, is maintained." Similar views have been voiced by some of the more strident American feminists as well.

A subtler and more irritating argument, but closely akin, is MacKinnon's contention that pornography reinforces an attitude in men toward women which feminists just don't like. In effect, these censors are seeking to rewrite the psychological and social rules in every private relationship between man and woman. In my mind they are vastly overstepping the bounds of permissible prescription. Besides, I am sure their thesis is wrong, or at least skewed. Some of the most Alan Alda–ish new men among my friends are secretly fond of pornography in which the man is the sole center of attention. Are they guilty of closet chauvinism? Do they feel that a partnership approach to marriage has compromised their masculinity? Maybe, somewhere deep down. But I suspect that the significant emotional impulse they feel is to find a fantasy world in which only their urges matter, and their hidden sin is not male chauvinism, but solipsism. It differs only in the degree of raw sensuality from all those best-selling romance novels for women.

None of this would matter very much to the public debate about elitism were it not for the social force that anything to do with sex, especially sexual violence, gives to an otherwise abstract argument. No polemic metaphor is more potent these days than the metaphor of rape.

The impact of this analogy is clear-cut in the social war of the sexes. Time and again, women have confused legitimate grievances such as harassment and the range of offenses labeled date rape with mere expressions of opinion that they do not happen to share. In one extreme but emblematic episode, a University of Michigan graduate student was ordered by his department not to display a small, discreet photo of his own wife, clad in a bikini, on his own desk in his own office because women colleagues viewed this as harassment of them rather than affection for his spouse. It does not take Freud to guess that they disapproved of what they assumed to be the character of his marriage and were intruding upon it to raise his consciousness.

The success of this demand is reflective of the truckling treatment of all minorities, especially at universities but increasingly in other elite sectors of society. Victims, which is to say anyone affiliated with any group that believes it has been victimized (except, of course, white heterosexual men), are deemed to have the right to determine how they are labeled, what may be said *to* them, and what may be said *about* them. In yet another academic echo of Marxism, administrators join activists in celebrating the importance of "community" over the importance of individual thought and exploration. Even in institutions ostensibly devoted to the life of the mind, freedom of speech is being dislodged by the perverse notion of freedom *from* speech. So-called "hate speech" codes are one egregious example; so are laws that unconstitutionally treat violence or harassment as worse when coupled with bigotry. But one need not defend racial epithets or sexual vulgarities as expressions of opinion to run afoul of this compulsory moralizing—one need only display a photograph of one's own spouse to someone who does not consider you, or her, liberated enough to eschew cheesecake snapshots.

Sexual dicta might seem remote from the concerns of this volume, but they are in fact among the most significant points of leverage in the attempted restructuring of how elite America works because of the symbolic equation many feminists draw between such male-linked societal values as competition and conquest and the ultimate male villainy of rape. This rhetorical overkill is meant above all, of course, to win arguments—or rather, in most cases, to head them off at the pass. Once the verbal stakes escalate to that bullying extent, reason flies out the window. But at a deeper level the aim of many feminists is to debunk the most basic fact of history—that the civilized and cultured world was built almost entirely by men, pursuing such male-defined aims as conquest and fulfilling such male urges as competition and aggression. Many feminist scholars squander their careers on attempts to assert that the world owes its shape to those who cooked and cleaned, or alternatively to unsung geniuses whose memories men conspired to erase (a not entirely incidental parallel to the more exaggerated claims of Afrocentrists).

Even among women prepared to accept the reality of the

past, one finds a widespread yearning to rewrite the rules of the present so that women may enjoy a more glorious future.

The overt goal of these feminists is to change ground rules of working life so that wives and mothers can, as the boast runs, "have it all." They argue that society benefits by giving special privileges to mothers in the marketplace. Is that so? Let me admit here that I think children are better off when their mothers (or fathers) stay home full-time, at least until the children enter school. I believe that much of the perceived educational decline of children has very little to do with the favorite whipping boy, television, and a great deal to do with a phenomenon that more closely fits the time frame of the decline—the two-income household, which in practice generally means employment for the mothers of young children. If this causal relationship holds true (and I readily concede that it is opinion rather than fact—if shared, albeit reluctantly, by virtually every working mother I know), then any benefit to society from the mother's working has to be weighed against the developmental loss to the next generation. Day care, the common solution, is usually merely custodial. The yuppie alternative, a live-in nanny, clearly represents an intellectual step down for the child. Of the ten parental couples to whom my wife and I are closest, eight have used live-ins, of whom not one had attended college (although the biological parents were mostly Ivy Leaguers) and only three were native speakers of English.

If we have swamped the schools by asking them to carry too many social burdens, might we not do the same to the economy? We have already made our businesses less free, and perhaps less competitive, by imposing the obligations of affirmative action for blacks, women, and assorted other minorities. If we add the necessity of being flexible in scheduling, pay, and promotion on behalf of mothers—plus the inevitable ill will that this is bound to cause among at least some nonmothers, male and female—the likely result is less efficiency, not more. There is, further, a question of fairness. Changing rules to accommodate those who try to combine parenthood and the workplace inevitably imposes a disadvantage—if only by taking away a competitive advantage—on those who don't. Why, pray, *should* an employee with divided loyalties be treated the same as one who will give his or her all to the job? And on the philosophical plane, how can the very people most apt to say that childbearing is a private matter when the subject is abortion then reverse themselves and insist that it is a societal matter when the subject is their personal need and convenience in the workplace?

Even so, such changes are ardently sought. They have become almost dogma in the mainstream of my Democratic party. The ideological push is coming from some highly influential places. In April 1992 the Yale Graduate School marked the centenary of its admission of women with a three-day symposium. The capstone was a speech by Wellesley College president Nannerl Keohane, a recipient of a 1967 doctorate in political science from Yale. She complained, with some legitimacy, that the very word *admit* suggests that women's participation at Yale was a benefice conferred by men (for which women presumably ought to be grateful) rather than a basic human right. This is a significant perception. Blacks feel much the same ambivalence about Lincoln and the Emancipation Proclamation, for it, too, suggests that they were "given" something to which they feel entitled as a matter of elemental dignity. It must be added, however, that the "right" of any or all women to be enrolled at a particular private university is much less evident in the language of the Constitution than the rights to work, vote, and enjoy other civil liberties made implicit in the Fourteenth Amendment.

Keohane asserted the existence of a glass ceiling throughout society, but based her evidence almost entirely on statistics concerning top universities. Those numbers are compelling at first glance. Women constitute half the enrollment at Yale

College, for example, and almost half the student body of the Yale Graduate School, yet they are only twenty-two percent of the faculty and just eleven percent of those with tenure. Those statistics are misleading, however, not only about the rest of America but also about the good intentions and accessibility of the ostensibly discriminatory universities. At the junior level of assistant professor, some forty-two percent of Yale's faculty are women. The combined effects of life tenure, a later average retirement age than in other fields, and a drastic shrinkage in senior staff positions (because of declining enrollment and straitened finances) have kept schools like Yale from moving women along into the senior ranks. While Keohane advocated one-for-one promotion, moreover, there are still a few elitists left who think that tenure and full professorship ought to go to the most distinguished scholars, regardless of race or gender. Does this concern for standards make them sexist bigots?

In truth, as Keohane acknowledged, bigotry and sexism are not the real problems. "The most primitive explanations for the glass ceiling are sociobiological. In our instinctual constitutions, women most of all want to have babies, and when the biological clock begins ticking in our thirties, our bodies realize this. No matter how ambitious or energetic we have been about our jobs, we inevitably resort back to nature."

Those years of ticking, it might be added, tend to coincide with the pivotal years in most careers—the tenure decision in universities, the partnership decision at law firms, the point where corporate or media comers move onto the fast track to the very top. To want it all is to want too much.

For Keohane, the solution is obvious, and the people who are to pay for it should be anyone but the direct beneficiaries:

There will need to be more flexibility in our expectations for how one performs in high-powered jobs at different stages of one's life, and also in the support systems for working parents.

More flexible timetables for coming up for tenure, or the chance to attain tenure as a part-time professor, as well as more generous child-care and leave provisions and other policies that recognize the actual circumstances of people's lives, could make a big difference in opening those blockages in the pipeline. Changes will occur only if people press for them, if desirable young working couples insist on such arrangements before they will accept employment [Does she mean a husband should use himself as a bargaining chip to sweeten his wife's career, another easy way to breed workplace resentment?] and if citizens press for changes in our laws and tax structures. . . . I spoke earlier of the "admitting" mind-set that dominated our thinking from 1892 until quite recently. The "incorporation" mind-set, by comparison, acknowledges and celebrates the fact that including women as full partners makes a difference in the tone and temper of any human community or enterprise.

This airy claim to competitive advantages, special bargaining rights, and unspecified tax benefits for those who make the private decision to have children is a blatant form of special pleading. The last two sentences of the speech, moreover, underscore the inherent illogic and inconsistency of Keohane's position, and by extension that of the countless feminists who side with her on this issue (or, as they see it, nonissue already beyond debate). To claim the right to admission, or rather "incorporation," women are purporting to be equivalent to men. But they do not want to play by the same rules as men; instead, they demand that the rules be rewritten solely to benefit working mothers (and, ostensibly, their husbands). Further, these women claim to be different from men in tone or temperament—and, by implication, better. While Keohane is prudent enough not to articulate the words directly, this smacks of the "communal" and "nurturing" claims made for women, black "sun people," and other minorities seeking an instantaneous moral basis on which to redistribute power and remake the very dynamics of public life.

In fairness to Keohane, there is a solid elitist argument to be made for reintegrating mothers into the work force as soon as possible. Educated women are an asset to society—"human capital," in the phrase Bill Clinton likes to toss around—and they ought, all things being equal, to be utilized as thoroughly as possible. This is the rationale for the "mommy track," the alternative career path (with admittedly lower expectations) that was widely being urged a few years ago until zealots renewed the call for having it all. It is also the rationale for the family leave bill, vetoed by President Bush but signed by Clinton, that compels employers to rehire staff who take extended leaves to fulfill emergency family responsibilities. While there is a more airtight case to be made for the optional mommy track than for the obligatory preservation of jobs during family leave, both are premised on the real world in which we live —a world in which women voluntarily take on a disproportionate share of domestic worries.

Feminists object to such arrangements on three grounds. First, they do not wish to validate what they see as an unequal sharing of the household burden, based on what they reject as stereotypical views of the roles of the sexes. Second, they see compromise as a betrayal of feminism's promise of unlimited options. Third, they see it as both possible and preferable to compel the public world to make compromises rather than expect individual families (meaning, in practice, just the women) to do so.

The choice between career and family is so painful that women would rather not make it—and feminist activists are offering the illusory promise that they will not have to. The truth is, however, that in our culture most of the jobs truly worth having, those that are stimulating and demanding and full of intellectual peril, cannot be confined to forty hours a week or anything remotely like it. Working mothers of young children can hardly accommodate themselves to the minimum demands, let alone the maximum and erratically scheduled demands of the best jobs. The ancillary mommy track is not a dismissal; it merely describes reality.

By this point, any woman still reading is probably wishing she could puncture my bombastic carcass with whatever is the contemporary equivalent of a hatpin. I freely confess to having paid no attention here, let alone obeisance, to the very real problem of sexual harassment (accompanied, it must be pointed out, by some surreal claims seeking to extend the definitional boundaries of that sin). I have paid little attention to the troubles of women who can't get into the most lucrative unions or who are paid, as secretaries, a mere fraction of what men get for driving buses or hauling garbage. The first concern of this volume is the elite. Blue-collar jobs are outside its purview.

I strongly support the concept of equal pay for equal work. I do not join in the feminist campaign for *equivalent* pay for *equivalent* work (as if it could be defined in a neutral, objective way). This "refinement" is meant to overturn the judging process of the free market because some people don't like its outcomes. There undoubtedly are elements of historical prejudice in the lower pay scales for jobs customarily taken by women. But in the world of today, no one obliges a woman to take any particular job—she can slop hogs, chase crooks, or peddle commodities options if she likes and can qualify—and the rest of us should not be penalized for a woman's free choice to do something that traditionally has been done mostly by women.

Is Susan Faludi right that a lot of men continue to resent the women's movement and to thwart the progress of particular women? Do some other men behave with less conscious, but sometimes just as destructive, insensitivity or ignorance? Absolutely. But the point is not any individual lapses from perfection. The point is whether the upper reaches of American society are functioning effectively and, if not, whether a communal, nurturing, and infinitely flexible management structure is the best way to fix things. For many feminists, tribalists, Marxists, and new agers, it is self-evident that such a structure is best. To them, that is the way the world ought to be. But in my experience of corporate life, executives and professionals already spend far too much time in meetings, feel-good sessions, and public relations exercises and far too little in actually turning out the product and getting it sold. "Human resources" issues, from alcohol treatment to affirmative action, already consume an immense amount of time and preclude many decisions, particularly on hiring and firing, that would get made swiftly and surely in a truly free market. I welcome women into the workplace—and they are there in their millions, with or without my welcome. But the last thing the country needs is to further encumber the economy with social burdens likely to raise costs and reduce competitiveness.

Wrongheaded as it may be when applied to remaking the American workplace, there is something attractive and even noble in women's global sense of sisterhood. One need not accept the argument that the world would be a better place if women ran it to concede that the spirit of humanism and compassion seems to run deeper among the female of the species than the male. This may simply be the converse of women's lesser ardor for competition and conquest. But a plausible case can be made that the aggressive qualities needed to build the modern world are rather less helpful in sustaining it.

Equally romantic, but not always so noble, is women's search for female "ancestors" who beat the odds and accomplished something. Contemporary women seem to draw confidence from the attainments, even minor ones, of women of the past, and as a result they are prone to exaggerate the scale of these achievements and to view them out of the context of the vastly more numerous and defining achievements of men. This is especially conspicuous in the study of humanities, particularly literature and the arts. A vast proportion of what passes for female scholarship is either overblown hagiography of minor figures proffered for rediscovery or "feminist critiques" meant to reinvent the past to suit the needs of the present.

A sure way to get published in academic circles these days, it seems, is to title your book *Feminism and . . .* or *Women and . . .* and fill in the blank with almost anything. Some recent favorites: *Blood Relations: Menstruation and the Origins of Culture; Sentimental Modernism: Women Writers and the Revolution of the Word;* and *Feminism and Geography: The Limits of Geographical Knowledge.* The first, published by Yale University Press, makes exactly the sweeping claims that the title implies, in prose that combines jaw-breaking grandiosity and fogbound speculation to "prove" that women, not men, invented civilization. A sample:

Shoreline-foraging Aboriginal women from earliest times phase-locked with the tides, and correspondingly conceptualized themselves as immersed once a month in a "flood" of blood-symbolised togetherness transcending the individuality of each participant. In their monthly menstrual immersion or sex strike . . . the participants would have felt their separate identities being transcended in that of the great kinship coalition which together they formed. . . . In principle, it would only have needed two females—perhaps sisters, perhaps mother and daughter—to have set in train the movement towards culture as an unstoppable force. If these two always backed each other up, always acted in concert, synchronized their menstrual cycles and were able to motivate two or more males to hunt for them by making sex dependent on it, then they might have been so much more successful in securing meat than other females in the population. . . .

The second, published by Indiana University Press, makes the literary case for writing that ranks just one cut above Harlequin romances:

In spite of feminist and postmodernist efforts, the position against the sentimental still operates almost like an unconscious in critical writing. . . . The degradation of sentimental writing, made to represent the emotional fakery of women's pleadings, has covered over the transgressive content of the sentimental, its connection to a sexual body, and its connection to the representations of consciousness.

The third, published so far as I know only in Britain but too deliciously daffy not to surface in the United States, offers "a sustained examination of the masculinism of contemporary geographical discourses." Among its rhetorical sallies:

Women's exclusion is not only a question of the themes of research, nor even of the new concepts with which feminists work to organize those themes, but rather a question related to the very nature of hegemonic geographical knowledge itself. . . . I argue that to think geography—to think within the parameters of the discipline—is to occupy a masculine subject position. Geography is masculinist. . . . After examining many of the founding texts of philosophy, science, political theory and history, feminists have argued that the notion of reason as it developed from the seventeenth century onwards is not gender neutral. On the contrary, it works in tandem with white bourgeois heterosexual masculinities.

I wish I could say, for the sake of America's daughters, that this whiny bilge is atypical. It's not.

Fortunately, some women scholars swim against the tide. In the realm of biography, Catherine Gallagher of the University of California at Berkeley has acutely observed in a discussion of Britain's first truly professional female author, Aphra Behn:

Feminist scholars of the recent past have been surprisingly slow to take a serious interest. She conforms to none of the grandly trans-historical theories about women and writing that were popular in the 1970s and early 1980s. For example, she did not take up the pen with fear and trembling, deeply impressed by its undoubted resemblance to a penis. Nor do her writings reveal a hidden female culture or firm bonds of solidarity between women. . . . In short, Behn took patriarchy too much in her stride and was therefore irrelevant to the critics of the 1970s who were looking for either psychic damage or ideological ancestors.

In the same piece, Gallagher makes the subtle and significant point that any biography or psychological reconstruction based on text itself is apt to be a mere act of projection on the part of the editor-interpreter. In choosing which of an artist's works to include, particularly one who was as prolific as Behn, the selection reflects the editor's understanding and then reinforces it in the mind of the reader. As Gallagher puts it succinctly: "This is only one of the plausible Aphra Behns that we could pull out of the complete poems."

Germaine Greer has taken such salutary debunking even further in a blistering review of collected facsimiles of *Poems by Ephelia,* purported by the publisher to be the work of a single unnamed female poet rather than, as Greer contends, any number of writers of either gender choosing a popular pseudonym of the time. Writes Greer:

The rationale behind the retrieval of scarce works by women is that scholars wish to find out how long-dead women felt and thought from how they wrote, but the authenticity of virtually all the texts can be questioned. Very few autograph manuscripts have survived; the versions we have have invariably been edited, corrected by a better-educated male friend, punctuated by a copyist or publisher, even, as in the case of Katherine Philips's letters, completely rewritten after the author's death. Though she might long to retrieve a female genius from the obscurities and distortions that prevent her recognition, the feminist scholar must control her longing and proceed with scrupulous care, if she is not to discredit herself and further distort her subject.

This, Greer witheringly argues, feminist scholar Maureen Mulvihill has failed to do, combining historical error, misreading of text, allegedly fuzzy genealogy, and other errors in order to produce an "ancestor" of note. Greer concludes: *"Poems by Ephelia* (c. 1679) should be in every university library as an object-lesson to research students in how not to proceed in a problematic case of Restoration attribution." The sad fact is that the book is more apt to be purchased as a model of how to find, or formulate, an "ancestor."

Among women academicians of a more abstract inclination, it is not surprising, alas, that so many have allied themselves to the school of scholarship that maintains that an author's intention is irrelevant—that any reading is legitimate and a subversive one is probably better. This sort of piffle is the easiest way to overlook or, preferably, overthrow the male dominance of the higher culture, particularly in Europe.

The unvarnished truth is this: You could eliminate every woman writer, painter, and composer from the caveman era to the present moment and not significantly deform the course of Western culture. Of course you would lose individual artists of merit: I'd sorely miss Jane Austen and George Eliot, Sigrid Undset and Willa Cather. But you would eradicate few if any true giants, and hardly anyone who radically changed a form instead of simply executing it well. I could expand on this assertion, but I doubt it is necessary. I have tried it out on several dozen male and female acquaintances who are learned and cultured, in most cases as a vocation, and they have all agreed with me, although each and every one asked not to be quoted. This does not mean women are inferior. It simply means they didn't have the opportunity. There should be no shame in this for modern women—and certainly no reason to feel that the works of Shakespeare, Rubens, and Beethoven should be less inspirational to young ladies than to young gentlemen. But this inescapable fact incenses many feminist scholars and has made them, in universities at least, the fiercest and most numerous enemies of elitism. If women cannot be numbered equally with men in the ranks of proven genius, if indeed hardly any women merit being studied at all on the basis of the quality of their work, then the concepts of genius and quality must be discarded as politically unacceptable. Indeed, the society that produced the works of high culture must be rejected for its sexism, and the men who made that culture must be damned for their complicity in the silence of women. Of all the insidious forms of political correctness, this kind of thinking seems to me the worst. The historical role of centers of learning has been to preserve standards and protect enduring achievements from the wind and fire of momentary political or populist whim. Now the professors are fanning the flames.

I don't want to suggest that there is nothing worth studying in the lives of women present or past. They are, after all, half the human race. While that does not mean that they should necessarily constitute half of all scholarly topics, either cumulatively or even at just the present moment, the most hardened male chauvinist would have to concede the significance of, say, the iconography of women in art, the place of women in a feudal or agrarian economy, and the evolving patterns of childrearing through the ages, to cite just a few fruitful areas of inquiry. Such studies can legitimately be taken up by scholars of either gender, although as a matter of both practicality and sentiment they are more apt to be chosen by women, who usually care more and who frequently greet male researchers in "their" terrain with suspicion and perhaps resentment.

The harder question is whether such topics ought to be

examined under the rubric of departments labeled "women's studies." One objection to such programs is that they do not constitute an area of sufficient scholarly apparatus to be pursued on their own. That may be true, but to say so is no longer politically tenable. Women understandably find it all but impossible to separate this question from that of the status and worth of women themselves. A better objection, but not much more viable these days, is that such programs isolate scholars and shred the grand fabric of inquiry. That is to say, they are tribal rather than integrationist and reject the melting-pot theory on which the rise of postwar American cultural, political, and economic power was based. Like other minorities, women of today do not want simply to be included. They want a piece of turf to call their own.

There are other, arguably more cynical motives for the feminist campaign. The very existence of women's studies departments provides both a rationale for feminist ideology and a place to develop and refine it. Administratively, the existence of such departments offers chairmanships, full professorships, and other career-advancing appointments that will automatically be set aside for women. In addition, the growth of such courses creates a guaranteed market for textbooks, which will again perforce be written by (and bring a resounding royalty income to) feminist women.

Without overstating the impact of universities, which are as much mirrors as makers of the larger society, one must recognize that the scholarly questions surrounding women's studies and feminist critiques are outshouted by politics. Lest you think I am overinterpreting, consider such ostensibly cultural works as *The Reenchantment of Art,* in which author Suzi Gablik writes: "The calculating, dominating male intelligence is opposed to the visionary, empathetic female principle, bound to the core of the universe." Or the "scholarly" conference topics cited scornfully by Camille Paglia in *Sex, Art and American Culture,* including an analysis of the significance of pink and blue "genderized" disposable diapers, the gender roles of shell collectors within the Philadelphia Concological Society, and the assessment of sexism in the layout of the New Jersey Turnpike, with its ramps and tollbooths, breakdown lanes and emergency phone system—"a man's road . . . constructed with no thought to the feminine view of reality." Or a review by Mary Jo Weaver in which she praises essayist Mary Daly's *Outercourse* for its "confrontations with rapacious patriarchy and her demanding calling to create a meta-patriarchal language." Weaver hails Daly as "intrepid . . . in the face of an exponentially increasing list of atrocities against women and the planet"—a list she does not bother to explicate. She refers to present-day life as "a world on the brink of self-destruction," although she does not explain how. The most shocking thing about this polemic masquerading as analysis is not that its author is a professor of religious studies and women's studies at Indiana University, but that it was published in the January 24, 1993, edition of that barometer of the mainstream, the Sunday *New York Times Book Review*.

Women trained in such programs as Weaver's, and arguably men trained at universities that have women's studies departments, are apt to go out into the world expecting to see opportunities specifically earmarked for the advancement of women. And they will find them aplenty.

Of these, affirmative action targets are the most obvious and pervasive but by no means the only examples. PBS now offers the weekly half-hour talk show *To the Contrary,* aired on more than two hundred stations, in which analysis of news and national affairs is conducted by an all-women panel. Women are not exactly invisible elsewhere in television news and public affairs, and no one would dream of offering an officially all-male show. But this series is sponsored by the mainstream-to-conservative Toyota USA and Sun Company and has aired virtually without objection to its exclusionary casting. Elsewhere, on cable, one finds the women-only talk show of Jane

Wallace and Mary Matalin, even though the need for a gender-identified talkfest is not so clear in a form dominated by Oprah, Joan, Sally Jessy, et al.

Jeopardy!, the only television game show that is premised on knowledge rather than gambling, guesswork, or holding opinions resembling the statistical norm, has been shuffling its selection of topics and questions to ensure that more women succeed. This may be merely the free market at work rather than reverse sexism; the show has more female than male viewers, and its producers want to be sure the audience can empathize with the winners. On the other hand, anyone interested in a game based on knowledge is presumably prepared to accept that a fact is a fact rather than a "masculinist" principle at work.

In Britain, the Labour party has voted to exclude male candidates from about forty parliamentary seats in an attempt to double the party's female share in the House of Commons. Under a decision adopted by the party's National Executive Committee in June 1993, half of all constituencies where a sitting member is retiring or where a seat held by another party is considered attainable will be instructed to have women-only shortlists. Explained Clare Short, who chairs the Executive's women's committee: "The number of women will gradually increase every Parliament until eventually there is fifty percent women." She predicted a future "psychological breakthrough where it becomes normal to have women MPs and people like women candidates." Apart from the rigidity of the scheme, one might question its timing, coming nearly fifteen years after Margaret Hilda Thatcher began to make herself the most successful British prime minister of the postwar era. The American electoral system precludes such quota setting. But in our elections—where, as California legislator Jesse Unruh famously observed, "Money is the mother's milk of politics"—the for-women-only Emily's List is now widely viewed as the most effective fund-raising and targeting organization. The National Organization for Women, which used to judge candidates on their ideology, bolted toward gender-based endorsements in 1993 when its New Jersey chapter backed moderate-to-conservative Republican Christine Todd Whitman rather than her much more liberal Democratic opponent, incumbent James Florio, almost entirely on the basis that she was a woman. (The sole additional proviso, it seemed, was that she take the "correct," i.e., pro-choice, position on abortion.)

"What do women want?" Freud asked in a letter to Marie Bonaparte in 1931. The answer, of course, depends on which women and in what country one does the asking. In China, women probably want an end to the prejudice that leads to vastly more abortions and infant deaths of girls than of boys. In India, they probably want an end to the dowry scams that treat daughters of marriageable age as burdens that families must buy their way out of. In Muslim Africa, some of them surely want an end to the genital mutilation of small girls to ensure their lack of interest in sex and consequent marital fidelity—and, of course, an end to the kind of patronizingly pro–third world scholarship that attempts to explain this butchery as a mere cultural custom, not to be meddled with by outsiders. In the Philippines and Thailand, women may want economic growth that will challenge prostitution as the only viably lucrative job open to them.

In America, women laudably want an end to all the indignities and injustices visited on their sisters around the world, and they want equality for themselves. But feminist rage masquerading as scholarship here won't do anything to change inhumanity elsewhere. Rejection of "rationalism" and its social and political fruits will make the American economy weaker, not stronger, and hence diminish women's benefits from it. Revamping the rules to give special opportunity to working mothers will heighten, not diminish, any residual male resistance. And mistaking equality of opportunity for equality of outcomes will amount to blinding ourselves to the very real ways in which women's lives are different—in which they are, if not more, certainly other than just "the female of man."

FIVE

Nature and Nurture

"Who ever said life was fair?"
—JOHN FITZGERALD KENNEDY

THE HARDEST PART of defending elitism is coming to terms with the random, amoral way in which both society's goods and the means of achieving them are distributed among individual people. Why are some brilliant and others dim? Why are some hale and hearty and others handicapped? Why are some deaf, some blind, some mute? And if "why?" proves unanswerable, at least in any way that resembles social justice, then what posture ought society to take about those at either extreme—the gifted and the shortchanged? This dilemma is of abiding interest to philosophers and theologians. But even for those unengaged by metaphysics, it poses four sets of intriguing questions.

The most basic group of them is economic. Every industrial society has accepted, to some degree, the notion of redistribution of wealth on behalf of the poor, the aged, the infirm, and the incapable. The ongoing debate is over the details: How much and for what? Is the goal merely to ensure survival of those unable to provide for themselves, or should one afford them a measure of comfort, even indulgence? Which of their medical and social needs are to be met? Should one spend on treatments or equipment designed to make them better adapted to society? What about spending to make society better adapted to them, from closed captioning of television programs to rendering buildings, streets, and subway systems wheelchair-accessible? Where possible, ought they be enabled to work, if need be by the creation of makework? Along with this set of questions about what claim the shortchanged may make on society also comes a mirror set about what claim society may make on the gifted.

In any taxation system based on income, especially any that is labeled "progressive," the bulk of the proceeds will be taken from those more than usually gifted (assuming one accepts the notion that pay has some close correlation to merit and achievement and that these attributes are considered "gifts" in the sense both of talents and of unearned good fortune). This is partly a product of practicality and partly a reflection of a widespread moral judgment that those who have been blessed should pay alms in thanksgiving.

But the precise degree to which such expectations are imposed—which is to say, the extent to which income redistribution is regarded as justified—is an outgrowth of other questions to be pursued later in this chapter: To what extent is economic success a product of inherited talent? How important are free will and personal responsibility in determining one's fate? Is the propensity of those from privileged backgrounds to succeed, and of those from impoverished backgrounds to fail, purely a product of social determinism, or do factors of individual choice and merit come significantly into play?

The second big group of questions centers on integration. As noted in Chapter Two, there is a renewed push across the nation to include even severely disabled children in regular classrooms. The deinstitutionalization of mental patients, launched in the 1970s and 1980s and continuing today, reflects the same principle of incorporating people into mainstream society to the maximum extent possible, with society left to learn how to cope with the differences. In really liberal circles, this kind of thinking applies even to criminals. Jails are rejected as mere academies for the teaching of more serious crime, while community-based placements are urged as providing better rehabilitation (punishment is an all but taboo consideration). The handling of the elderly is the one notable exception to this trend. Nursing homes and other kinds of assisted or supervised living remain vastly more popular than sheltering aged relatives under one's own roof, even among the most exuberant advocates of general integration, perhaps because the personal sacrifices involved are real rather than rhetorical.

A third set of questions has to do with nomenclature and the social contract. The crippled have become the handicapped and now the differently abled. A wheelchair-bound person has become one who *uses* a wheelchair (that language is deemed to make him or her sound less passive). AIDS victims have become People With AIDS. In one of the most extreme versions, those born deaf have altered from being hearing-impaired to "having a birthright of silence." Every bit of plain speaking offends someone these days. When I metaphorically described the dancing in the ill-fated Broadway musical *Nick and Nora* as "clubfooted" in a review in *Time,* I predicted to the copy editor involved that we would get a letter from some organization for the clubfooted, objecting that this nomenclature implied a deformity—and I was right. My review of Stephen Sondheim's *Assassins* bore a headline that spoke of the killers and would-be killers of American presidents as "loony," which the vast majority of them irrefutably were. This prompted a two-page single-spaced letter from a spokeswoman for the insane, protesting that the reference to the mental state of these deranged shooters was unfair to the crazy. More recently I was struck by a lawsuit filed on behalf of a mentally retarded eighth-grader in Dayton, Ohio, whose guardian wanted the girl to be able to attend a prom limited to high school students. Noting that her daughter was the same age as some others eligible to attend and asserting that the girl could exercise comparable judgment, Thelma Sell said, "Sherrie is handicapped. She's not stupid." If she is not "stupid," then what exactly does mentally retarded mean?

I find personal amusement in the proliferation of groups denouncing "sizism," which means bias against the over-

weight, and "looksism," which means bias against the unat-
tractive. Having been up to a hundred pounds overweight for
most of the past fifteen years, and having been married nearly
all of that time to a woman who was the same (she has since
become a lean and hungry health club fanatic), I know the
terrain. Two facts are indisputable. First, whatever their other
medical problems, fat people are fat because they eat too
much. They may have slow metabolisms and therefore need to
eat much less than others. But however much or little they
eat, it is more than they need to sustain them at an optimal
weight. And second, when prospective employers wonder
whether a fat person may be less nimble and more apt to get
sick, they are merely showing common sense. It is true that
boorish men (and sometimes women) are apt to make remarks
about weight to complete strangers. But there are limits to our
ability to wish away rudeness, particularly in an area that in-
tersects with the volatile and private realm of sexual attraction.

The fourth set of questions has to do with amelioration and
change. If society accepts a duty to make things better for the
unfortunate, does it have a concomitant right to do so
whether or not the intended beneficiaries seek or even desire
the help? In the coldest part of winter, many of the homeless
—particularly those with emotional problems—refuse to be
housed in shelters. They stay outdoors, where some of them
freeze to death. Some schizophrenics of my acquaintance pe-
riodically refuse to take medication that helps control their
problems because they prefer the way they feel when they are
more detached from reality.

The impulse in current American society is to "empower"
the afflicted, even to the extent of engaging in the charade
that they suffer no affliction but are merely somehow different. At some point this exchange between the more fortunate
person and the less fortunate one transits from a mildly condescending pretense to a folie à deux.

A striking example is the ongoing assertion among the deaf

that theirs is simply an alternative culture, as rich and varied and valid as anyone else's. The more extreme among them oppose the installation of hearing implements or restorative surgery as an insulting intrusion. They reject having children learn English as early as possible and instead urge emphasizing their own American Sign Language. Perhaps ASL is as vibrant and nuanced a language as its advocates claim; I don't know it, and the handful of my acquaintances who do all learned it as hearing adults, long after mastering English. But I do know two things. First, ASL cannot possibly be as nuanced and subtle as English, which has many, many more words and a greater potential for sensitivity (ASL speakers indicate homosexuals with a swish of the wrist and denote Asians by making gestures around the eyes to indicate a slant). Second, English is the language of American government, commerce, and education, and someone who remains primarily dependent on ASL is probably doomed to stay within his or her "culture," perhaps in the self-perpetuating role of teaching ASL to the next generation. In arguing that deaf children are happier without cochlear implants to help them hear and without early emphasis on English to help them communicate across the hearing barrier, deaf militants are in effect saying that these children are better off asserting equal but alternate status than they are in admitting their limitations and learning as much as they can. One hears echoes of the similar extremism among Afrocentrists and feminists; if we can't have our culture and historical status validated as equal, then let's abandon the whole process of comparison. In my mind, partial failure is always better than delusory success.

If the discontented were engaging in this self-deception on their own as an exercise in the power of positive thinking, it might not seem so troubling. But when they persuade the larger society to go along with them, they promote at minimum a tawdry hypocrisy and at worst a further erosion of the competitive spirit. In some instances, they also cost society an immense amount of money in pursuit of a sometimes chimerical principle. Three incidents are illustrative.

As mentioned in the opening chapter, in November 1992 a deaf and mute high school student won the right to enter an annual speech contest sponsored by the Veterans of Foreign Wars. (That year's topic, ironically in the circumstances, was "My Voice in America's Future.") She pursued her case in a federal district court and withdrew only after the VFW agreed to admit her and proffered an abject apology. The rules of the contest require entrants to submit audiotapes of themselves delivering their speeches. The tapes are identified only by number during the judging process in an attempt to weed out personal sympathies and prejudices among the evaluators. Instead, the judges weigh two factors: the content of the speech, as written in English, and the oratorical style of its delivery.

The would-be entrant, Shannon Merryman of Bristol, Rhode Island, proposed to meet neither requirement. She demanded that she be permitted to submit a videotape—something no other contestant is allowed to do—in which she would "speak" in American Sign Language. The presentational elements of oratory, the seductive and persuasive and inspirational capacities of the human voice, would perforce be lacking from her submission; even the use of her hands in gesture would have little to do with traditional oratory, for she would be conveying literal information rather than reinforcing her words by emphasis and metaphor. Moreover, Merryman's chosen language of ASL is not English; it is not even a literal translation of English, but has its own grammar. No reasonable person wants to deny the handicapped the right to compete with the rest of the world to the full extent that it is possible. But what Merryman proposed to do was not to compete at the same activity. Rather, she wanted to do something altogether different and have it be treated as the same thing.

After the contest's administrators declined her proposal,

Merryman went public and the political results were predictable. When a sixteen-year-old girl with a disability is pitted as a female David against a Goliath-size organization of older, mostly white, and largely conservative men, in the court of public opinion the David is bound to win. Howard Vander Clute, the VFW's adjutant general and head of its national headquarters, ultimately denied any intention to discriminate and blamed the whole fuss on bureaucracy. "I'm not sure where the communication broke down," he said. "I think the reason it went to court was that someone felt it should have been addressed before."

The organization did salvage a fig leaf to place over its retreat. Instead of a videotape, Merryman agreed to submit an audiotape in which her ideas would be translated by an interpreter. But Merryman vowed to renew her bid to speak for herself, in ASL, in a future installment in the contest. Her mother added, "We don't want to just drop this. We want to see things change so that people will be able to accept people who are not quite the same." In fact, of course most Americans are prepared to do that now. What Merryman was really asking was that people accept her as being "quite the same" when she is not. There are many things deaf-mute people can do. Oratory is not, however, among them.

The second instructive episode dates from the 1970s, when the District of Columbia was in the final stages of completing its subway system, the Metro. For whatever reasons—construction techniques, insensitivity, mere oversight—at least some of the stations were ready to receive physically normal passengers many months before they would be ready to accommodate the handicapped. Officials apologized and offered interim solutions, including unlimited free taxi rides for any handicapped people who requested them. This was on its face a far better deal than actual use of the system, and if the handicapped had been smart, they would have proposed that it be made permanent. It was cheaper, it was safer, and it was bound to be more convenient because it would be door to door. But no. The handicapped insisted on keeping the system closed to everyone until it was fully accessible to them, prompting one exasperated scholar of my acquaintance (a prominent Ivy League liberal who would strangle me for using his name) to snort publicly about "crippo liberation." (One feels inclined to put in this same category the decision of the Los Angeles city disabled commission to shut down a nude "shower dancing" attraction at a cabaret, not because the entertainment was lewd but because it was inaccessible to performers and customers in wheelchairs. This may, however, have been an instance of puritanism merely masquerading as political correctness.) Of course the handicapped are right to insist on having an opportunity to do everything that everyone else can, including commute to work. But it flies in the face of reality to insist that they ought always to be able to do everything in exactly the same *way* as everyone else.

The third illustrative episode came in August 1992, when the Bush administration rejected Oregon's plan to ration health care. The plan involved numerically ranking treatments and services by their likelihood to prolong or improve life and barring Medicaid payment for roughly the bottom twenty percent. Some treatments, such as therapy for the common cold, were barred because they were not necessary. Others, such as treatment for traumatic brain injury or for AIDS patients believed to be in the last six months of life, were excluded because they were expensive and unlikely to do much good. Some, such as liver transplants for people with alcoholic cirrhosis, seemed to be ruled out as a moral judgment that the patient had brought his problem on himself and a practical judgment that his behavior might well recur. Perhaps the toughest and most unpopular decision was to withhold payment for cancer treatments for patients whose prospects of surviving at least five years were less than ten percent. In the face of cancer, most Americans believe a patient should be entitled to try anything, regardless of how high the cost or how low the likelihood of success—as was evidenced by the epochal $77 million jury award in December 1993 to the heirs of a California woman who was denied money for a highly experimental late-stage cancer treatment (which she then financed privately and which failed anyway). Although most of the excluded conditions in Oregon were diseases, at least some, such as foot deformities and certain kinds of epilepsy, were disabilities. AIDS, although a disease syndrome, also has been officially labeled a disability, thus affording its sufferers a broad range of legal protections.

In denying Oregon's proposal, Secretary of Health and Human Services Louis W. Sullivan asserted that the rankings were based on the premise that "the value of the life of a person with a disability is less than the value of a life of a person without a disability." That presumption, he added, would violate the Americans with Disabilities Act. The core issue, of course, is value to whom. The life of a disabled person is worth an infinite amount to him or her; it is the only one he or she has. But its value to society is by definition finite. Even if we do not place caps on medical treatment, we do on subsistence and "entitlement" payments. Oregon officials had the courage to make choices. As Oregon's Democratic congressman Ron Wyden pointed out, the Bush administration chose in a reelection year to be "politically safe." While American society is clearly not ready to confront legislation or administrative regulations that question the value of those no longer sentient at either end of life—severely retarded children and elderly people in a chronic coma—the time may be coming when we face up to a basic economic reality. Almost everything anyone proposes to spend public money on is in some sense worthwhile. But there is not enough money to do everything, and as technology improves, the gap will only widen. Modern medicine does not simply make more people healthy. Its larger effect is to keep more chronically sick people alive. At some point the elitist impulse must be recognized as the only tenable one: to say, at least by the inaction of withholding treatment, that some lives are indeed worth less to society than others. Ideologues will denounce this as fascism. It is really just candor.

When John Kennedy asked rhetorically about the fairness of life, he knew whereof he spoke. He had been born attractive, intelligent, and wealthy. He grew up in a family of glamour and political power. He survived the war that took the lives of so many of his contemporaries, and emerged a certified hero to boot. His family connections helped him win a Pulitzer Prize (and his employees may have helped him write the volume for which he was honored). He got away with massive amounts of marital infidelity, including an affair with a girl-friend whom he shared with Mafiosi, and he managed to conceal medical conditions that might have raised grave doubts about his fitness for the rigors of the White House.

When John Kennedy asked rhetorically about the fairness of life, he knew whereof he spoke. His father was a philan-derer and both parents were often away. His older brother was killed in war. A sister died in a plane crash. Another sister was mentally retarded. He endured severe back pain and kidney problems. He and his wife lost a newborn child. A taint of alleged vote fraud in Chicago will forever cloud his greatest triumph, being elected President. And he had his brains blown out in front of a watching world at the age of forty-six.

Depending on how you look at things, Kennedy's life and most others can seem either unjustly harsh or unjustly soft. Not surprisingly, most of us have days when we are thrilled to be alive and days when we halfway wouldn't mind being hit by a truck.

One of the classic restoratives for those dispirited days is to catch a glimpse of someone worse off. "I mourned that I had no shoes," the proverb runs, "until I met a man who had no feet." As a reminder of one's good fortune, such exposure is salutary. For this reason, I used to make a point of taking a vacation somewhere in the third world at least once every couple of years, to refresh my awareness of how fortunate the most workaday, middle-of-the-middle American is by global standards.

The problem in contemporary America is that our awareness of life's capriciousness has translated into guilt whenever things go well. The mass media and the political tactics they have bred (lobbying, demonstrations, press conferences, and photo opportunities) have made us all much more aware of the disadvantaged. We have responded not just with compassion, but also with deep self-doubt. Winners no longer feel they have a right to exult in their victories. Losers no longer feel so responsible for the depth of their defeat, regardless of the facts of the case. Self-proclaimed victims of society have lost sight of the proportion of their fate that reflects free will. Too often, people who grasp that they are not responsible for certain aspects of their problems decide that they can legitimately be irresponsible about every aspect of their problems. Just as often, their betters are prone to let them do so and to commiserate over the sad results.

A pointed example of this social dynamic is the success of the musical play *Blood Brothers,* which has had two long runs in London's West End and which is, as I write, in its fourteenth month on Broadway. In America it has survived as an "audience" show despite what would normally be killing reviews. The premise is that twin brothers are born to an impoverished working-class woman and that just one of them— for contrived reasons—is adopted into a middle-class home. The middle-class boy grows up to be attractive, athletic, wholesome, bright, and impeccably mannered. The working-class boy—who is the *hero!*—grows up scruffy, coarse, idle, and disruptive. He drinks. He steals. He sleeps around. He scorns authority, falls in with thugs, and eventually commits murder. Every single one of these acts is portrayed not as his own fault or folly, but as the moral burden of the middle class.

I can imagine that readers who are unfamiliar with the show are by now assuming that what makes it popular is its score, or some trick of stagecraft, or some bravura performance while the political message slides by. Believe me, the sermon cannot be overlooked. In fact, as my wildly enthusiastic companion for a matinee—himself a Broadway veteran and TV series regular—readily conceded, the show's execution borders on the amateurish. My friend liked it, he explained, because he believes that it reflects the way the world really is. For half an hour after the curtain fell, he argued passionately that intelligence is equally distributed across class lines and that in most cases only the facts of one's upbringing determine whether one fails or succeeds. He rejected out of hand the idea that however hard the working-class boy's life had been, the choices he made—beginning with rejecting school—were entirely and culpably his own. Perhaps predictably, my exasperated friend called me an elitist.

The hard factual evidence on social mobility in America, like the evidence on most other divisive questions, is capable of being read whichever way you like. During the Reagan years, Democrats are fond of pointing out, the middle class—defined as those with incomes ranging between seventy-five percent and one hundred twenty-five percent of the national median—substantially shrank. In consequence, the gulf between the well-off and the ill-off widened. All that is true. But the reason the gulf widened is that a sizable chunk of the middle class advanced to the upper middle, with incomes beyond one hundred twenty-five percent of the norm. If America moved a bit closer to being a country divided between rich and poor, it was not because the ranks of the poor were increasing.

During this period the median American was surely upwardly mobile. Over the course of a lifetime, the median

American has absolutely been upwardly mobile, because national wealth has greatly increased while the pattern of concentration has shifted only marginally. As for the volume of individual movements up (or down) by amounts considerably greater than the norm, they are hard to quantify. But we know anecdotally that they happen often enough to be considered more than mere flukes. Indeed, we don't need to look much farther than Bill Clinton to find a telling example.

The problem of free will sheds light on an intriguing conundrum about the ideological differences between liberals and conservatives. It is a commonplace observation that liberals believe in the perfectibility of man while conservatives believe in the endurance of original sin. Superficially, that would suggest that conservatives take a more understanding and indulgent view of individual lapses, while liberals take a more harshly judgmental one. In fact, we know, quite the opposite is the case. Much as conservatives may be resigned to the unattainability of moral perfection, they delight in rewarding individual surges toward (or punishing individual retreats from) that state of grace. Liberals, on the other hand, assume that this moral nirvana will be reached collectively rather than by individual striving. In the real world, therefore, liberals tend to treat moral lapses as the collective fault of society.

If the goal of elitists is to distinguish confidently between better and worse cultures, better and worse ideas, better and worse contributions to society, then surely that judging process must extend to distinguishing between better and worse behavior. On the matter of free will and personal responsibility, even lifelong liberals of an elitist bent are forced to find common cause with conservatives. It is not that the downtrodden do not need or deserve help. It is that they will not have better lives until they are prepared on their own to embrace better values, not the least of which is self-reliance.

Much of the erosion in the sense of personal responsibility

among the poor can be traced, I think, to the late 1960s, when the language of "entitlement" began to become pervasive in American culture. That was the era as well of the National Welfare Rights Organization, a now-defunct lobbying group that had lasting importance chiefly because of the use of the word *rights* in its title. As late as the enactment of Lyndon Johnson's war on poverty programs just a few years before, it was generally accepted that welfare and other benefices from the state were not rights but charity, given voluntarily for the physical succor of the recipient and the moral succor of the donor. This sense of a voluntary transaction, one that might legitimately be terminated at any time, surely awakened at least some recipients to the awareness that they were ultimately responsible for their own fate. Once welfare became labeled a "right" or "entitlement," that change in rhetoric inevitably eroded the sense of personal duty to survive and improve.

A comparable effect has resulted, I suspect, from the rhetorical and actual emphasis on criminals' rights, indeed on all individuals' rights vis-à-vis "the state"—which in economic terms always means other individuals, who pay the bills. It is fashionable these days to deride Calvinism as having been a force for smugness of the comfortable and dismissal of the afflicted. But if one strips away the theological component, early Calvinists left us a residue of acute perception. In general, the world is a rational place in which winners on the whole deserve to win and losers deserve to lose. It is only for the exceptions, the lives that are strikingly unfair, that we maintain the mediating devices of social welfare.

In moral terms, it is probably irrelevant whether intelligence is largely a product of nature or largely a product of nurture. Either way, it is an accident of birth for which the beneficiary can claim credit only to the degree that he or she cultivates and disciplines a natural gift. To me it has always been self-evident that intelligence is primarily inborn. Anyone who has ever witnessed the birth of a litter of kittens or puppies knows that distinct differences in personality—curiosity, venturesomeness, and the like—are evident from the very moment of arrival into the world. If that is so in less complex organisms, how can it not be so in mankind, where personality varies so much more widely? Logic, moreover, impels us to believe either that intelligence is genetically linked or that Darwin was an utter chump. Assume that he was right in thinking that we evolved from a primate ancestor in the direction of intelligence for a hundred thousand generations. How and why should that process have abruptly halted in the middle of the twentieth century, precisely at the convenient moment for the egalitarian left?

The problem with a genetic basis for intelligence—or, more precisely, a genetic basis for economic success, which is what really provokes envy—is that we don't know what to do with it politically. The egalitarian principle underlying most of our social programs, and more pertinently their self-evaluation mechanisms, is that talent is evenly distributed across lines of class, race, and gender and that talent is, or should be, the primary determinant of economic success. If that is so, then a social program can be judged to have succeeded only when life outcomes are more or less equal across these lines. (All but a few extremists are prepared to make some slight allowance for the impact of parenting, neighborhoods, and the like.) If talent is distributed unequally, however, we have no useful means of measuring whether a program is doing any good or, alternatively, whether it amounts to just throwing money at a problem. If intelligence is genetically linked, moreover, then not only the children of the inner cities and rural backwaters, but *their* children as well, may be by and large doomed to economically stunted lives. Indeed, as low-skill jobs either dwindle in relative wages or disappear outright to automation or to competition overseas, the prospects of this next generation may in fact be even worse.

Some extraordinary people do rise from the ranks of the poor, and a prudent society should maximize their opportunities. What propels nearly all of these surprise achievers, however, is not just brains but an acute sense of being responsible for their own destinies. Indeed, a case can be made that responsible individualism should be considered a component of intelligence. It is the most adaptive practical response to the world in which we live.

Let us assume for a moment that America one day reaches egalitarian heaven, with absolutely equal distribution of wealth and social position across the board. Barring the dead hand of Marxism at the tiller, the economic stratification so deplored by the left would set in again almost immediately—because intelligence varies genetically and because intelligence by and large determines economic success. It is the nature of human society to be stratified. And it is this elitist tendency, far more than theories about heredity, that rankles egalitarians. The idea that life has winners and losers—that something inherent in individuals leads some to create and amass and others to thumb-twiddle and squander—offends egalitarians' sense of fair play. Their outlook reminds me of a nature videotape that I saw being hawked on television as I wrote this chapter. Billed as *Great Escapes,* the tape consists entirely of animals that are normally preyed upon instead escaping from larger or fiercer predators. "If you love underdogs," the announcer intones, "then this tape is for you." The worldview of the tape conveniently omits the bloody fact that carnivorous predators must kill or starve. The way of nature is combat and conquest, not nurturing communalism.

One of the most illustrative examples of how politics distorts debate about nature and nurture is the situation of homosexuals. The topic may seem slightly divergent from the rest of this chapter. Homosexuality has not been shown to be linked to intelligence, although those willing to be identified as gay in surveys typically report somewhat more formal education than the national average. (This may mean only that professionals and managers feel more secure economically and more willing to absorb the risks that come with being known as gay.) Similarly, homosexuality is not a physical handicap or deformity, although it is a difference that undeniably carries with it some significant social inconvenience.

A generation ago it was widely considered wicked to suggest that homosexuals might be genetically or biologically identifiable; this would imply that they were sports of nature, somehow misconceived or deformed. In those days the benevolent posture was to assert that their orientation was entirely a product of nurture, that they had been psychologically warped through no fault of their own.

Now the pendulum has swung and the widely fashionable view is that gays are indeed genetically different and ought to be accepted as foreordained products of God or nature. To suggest that early upbringing plays any noteworthy part in their adult behavior is to suggest that they are mentally sick or morally deficient and that their lives are "unnatural."

Plainly these analyses are mutually exclusive—although the influences they describe may both play a role in actual behavior. But as with most arguments over nature and nurture, intellectual rigor is secondary to emotional impulse. Whichever rationale one favors, the purpose of articulating it has been to defend homosexuals as natural or to denounce them as unnatural. In truth, the evidence for either view is sketchy and speculative. Moreover, no single explanation is apt to suffice to explain the behavior of hundreds of millions of people in today's world and countless others in centuries past. Indeed, the very category of homosexual is argued by some scholars to be a modern construct. In the ancient and medieval world, they say, a man's sexuality was defined by what acts he performed rather than with whom.

Interestingly, the question of free will has become central to the moral debate over homosexuality. Gay men and women assert that their orientation is not a choice. Conservative critics counter that behavior is always a choice: Having yearnings is not the same thing as acting upon them. At another level, the debate involves a moral equivalent of elitism and egalitarianism. Homosexuals say they should be as free as heterosexuals to act upon their impulses with other consenting adults; this is an egalitarian assertion. Their elitist opponents argue that heterosexuals should be more free because their way is better. On this issue, I find myself siding with the egalitarians, because the opposition to gays seems to boil down to squeamishness, narrowmindedness, and religious intolerance. But for the purposes of this book, the most interesting thing is simply to note how pervasive the language and logic of elitism versus egalitarianism has become.

It would be not merely infuriating to liberals, but discreditingly naive, for me to close this chapter without acknowledging that there are other factors besides intelligence that determine economic success. The playing field is not level. The children of the prosperous live in safer and healthier homes, by and large; they enjoy somewhat more stable family environments; they attend better schools and are surrounded by brighter and better-motivated classmates.

Beyond all this, successful youths may use tactics not altogether unfamiliar to the most unsavory of the poor. Quite often, they cheat. A survey of undergraduates at the Massachusetts Institute of Technology, where the academic standards are as high as anywhere and where the bulk of the studies are objective and numerical, found that more than eighty percent of them admitted having cheated in some fashion at least once during college. More than two thirds said they had committed some form of plagiarism. Nearly half had misrepresented or fudged data in a lab report or research paper. Is MIT a hotbed of immorality? Not by comparison with other schools, alas. A Rutgers University professor who surveyed fifteen thousand students at thirty-one major universities found that sixty-seven percent of humanities majors admitted cheating at least once during their college years.

What are we to make of such admissions? Are the accomplished to be reassessed as undeserving? Or are the pressures in universities too great, the demands and standards too high, so that the occasional lapse is only to be expected? Are we decaying into a society so forgiving of dishonor, so ready to accept almost anyone as a victim, that women and minority students feel entitled to take advantage and white men feel beleaguered into a perverse form of self-defense?

Or is all this simply a product of an educational system so egalitarian, so anti-elitist that even the elite don't learn what they need to learn?

There is troubling evidence for this latter view. Another survey, conducted among 3,119 students at the eight Ivy League schools, found that fifty percent could not name their own two U.S. senators, fifty-nine percent could not name as many as four justices of the Supreme Court, forty-four percent could not name the speaker of the House of Representatives, and thirty-six percent did not know that the speaker follows the vice president in the line of succession. While a less alarming eleven percent did not know who wrote the Declaration of Independence, fully seventy-five percent did not recognize the phrase "government of the people, by the people, and for the people" as having been spoken by Abraham Lincoln. (It is, of course, from the finale of the Gettysburg Address.)

None of this is quite as jarring, however, as what happened when a Stockholm newspaper gave five stock analysts the equivalent of $1,250 each and had them compete as investors for a month. The winning analyst, publisher of a newsletter, pushed his holdings up an impressive ten percent. But the contest also included a chimpanzee, who chose his stocks by throwing darts—and improved his portfolio by fifteen percent.

I view all these as cautionary tales that life is not only unfair but often unprincipled. Oscar Wilde was on to something when he wrote, "The good end happily and the bad unhappily. That is the meaning of *fiction.*" Any system that holds the downtrodden wholly responsible for their sorrowful fate is plainly defective. So, equally, is any system that does not demand of people that they make the most they can of their circumstances. In the delicate calibration of elitist toughness and egalitarian compassion, however, elitism ought to win out for two reasons. It directs society's resources where they have the most chance of stimulating growth and change and making a better life for everyone. And it keeps the pressure on every individual capable of self-improvement to be better than he used to be and to think more about that than about how someone else is always and unjustly going to be better still.

SIX

The Museum of Clear Ideas

"The much-esteemed Gibbon and his Virginian colleagues by cheerful error calculated that civilization motored a tidy upward turnpike to culminate in the city of Guess Who's worldly intelligence. But from A.D. 300, for a millennium, every daughter knew less than her mother, every son less than his father. Now, as we dispute over the exact moment when we engaged this autobahn downward again—hurtling in a tinny Cadillac fueled by idleness, greed and superstition —our great-grandfathers (the ones who could read and write) drape themselves white to hear our diminished chicken-cackle language in the parliament of fools."

—DONALD HALL, *The Museum of Clear Ideas: New Poems,* 1993

WHAT HAS BEEN the biggest social change in the United States since the end of World War II? A solid case can be made for the economic transition from the Depression, when privation was common and fear of it almost universal, to an era of plenty in which home ownership, two-car households, and retirement pensions are unremarkable norms. Equally, one could argue for the workplace emancipation of women—or, closely allied, the emergence of reliable birth control and the legalization of abortion, which together have allowed women much greater control over their economic as well as social destiny. In terms of human decency, it would be hard to name any social change more meaningful than the opening of doors to blacks. In terms of the literal face of the nation, it would be hard to define anything more potent than the expansion in legal immigration by nonwhite races and the bureaucratic blind eye generally turned toward illegal immigration by those same peoples. For smaller but intensely committed groups of Americans, the biggest if not necessarily most welcome change may seem to be the rise of gay rights or the awakening of environmental awareness or the wide legitimation of bilingualism.

Less obvious in the headlines, but at least as profound as any of these changes, has been the emergence of mass higher education. While all the major social changes in postwar America reflect egalitarianism of some sort (even environmentalists base their appeal on equality of rights among species), no social evolution has been more willfully egalitarian than opening the academy. Despite the seeming elitism of fostering self-improvement and learning, the true effects have been to help break down the distinctions between the accomplished and the workaday, and to promote pseudo-scholarship based on gender anxiety and ethnic tribalism.

Although political correctness outside the classroom and multicultural and feminist orthodoxy within it legitimately dominate the attention the public gives to universities these days, the really striking long-term changes at these institutions have to do with sheer size. Half a century ago a high school diploma was a significant credential, and college was a privilege for the few. Now high school graduation is virtually automatic for adolescents outside the ghettos and barrios, and college has become a normal way station in the average person's growing up. No longer a mark of distinction or proof of achievement, a college education is these days a mere rite of passage, a capstone to adolescent party time.

Some sixty-three percent of all American high school graduates now go on to some form of further education, according to the Department of Commerce's 1991 *Statistical Abstract of the United States,* and the bulk of those continuing students attain at least an associate's degree. Nearly thirty percent of high school graduates ultimately receive a four-year baccalaureate degree. A quarter or so of the population may seem, to egalitarian eyes, a small and hence elitist slice. But by world standards this is inclusiveness at its most extreme—and its most peculiarly American. For all the socialism of British or French public policy and for all the paternalism of the Japanese, those nations restrict university training to a much smaller percentage of their young, typically ten to fifteen percent. Moreover, they and other first world nations tend to carry the elitism over into judgments about precisely which institution one attends. They rank their universities, colleges, and technical schools along a prestige hierarchy much more rigidly gradated —and judged by standards much more widely accepted—than we Americans ever impose on our jumble of public and private institutions. This is not to say we don't have our own notions about the relative snob value of various schools; we just don't all share the same notions as consistently or value them as intensely. While there are families who will undertake any conceivable sacrifice to send their children to the most prestigious schools they can get into, there are as many who think the state university will do just fine because it's cheaper.

In the sharpest divergence from American values, countries such as Britain, France, and Japan tend to separate the college-bound from the quotidian masses in early adolescence, with scant hope for a second chance. For them, higher education is logically confined to those who displayed the most aptitude for lower education. We may view these siftings-by-exam with sentimental horror. We may take pride that, of late, some of these educationally elitist countries seem to be moving toward our style of inclusion and repechage. But the changes elsewhere probably reflect pandering populist politics more than economic rigor, just as they would here. These nations know full well that while pursuing their more elitist approach to education, they shared in the unparalleled postwar global economic boom just as much as America—and did so despite having been bombed into devastation, while we emerged from four years of war more or less industrially intact.

In today's United States, the social value of mass higher education is generally considered so obvious as to be beyond discussion. It is reflexively credited with having produced a better work force, a more stable electorate, a more flexible economy, a more civilized culture. It is considered an emblem of fairness. And it has certainly fed the national appetite for belief in betterment. If each generation is supposed to be more fortunate than the one preceding it, no symbol sums up that process of advancement more convincingly to the common man than having the first-ever member of one's own clan cross the great divide and enroll in college. Indeed, the college experience has come to be thought of as so much a right of citizenship that in February 1994 a New York City high school girl publicly asked her new mayor, Rudy Giuliani, in apparent sincerity, why there could not be scholarships unconnected with grades or merit, so that she and others like her could have the experience of going elsewhere to live on a campus rather than having to commute from home.

While it may be easy to laugh off this girl's demands for subsidized wanderlust, her notion that scholarly benefits should be unconnected to grades was actually embraced by New York's city university system during its "open enrollment" era, and it is de facto policy in many places today, particularly in the proliferating community (nee "junior") college system. This applies even at state universities, the top tier of the public system. Fully a fifth of them are required to accept any in-state high school graduate who seeks to enroll. If college used to be a reward for doing well in high school, it may now be a reward merely for having completed high school; that in turn may be a reward simply for having shown up, or for having grown too tall to be kept back.

The best reasons for skepticism about mass higher education, however, reach far beyond the decline in meaning of a degree. The opening of the academy's doors has imposed great economic costs on the American people while delivering dubious benefits to many of the individuals supposedly being helped. The total bill for higher education is about one hundred fifty billion dollars per year, with almost two thirds of that spent by public institutions run with taxpayer funds. Private colleges and universities also spend the public's money. They get grants for research and the like, and they serve as a conduit for subsidized student loans—many of which are never fully repaid, either because of forgiveness programs to foster community service or, more commonly, because of outright default. While the net amount taken from taxpayers is considerably less than one hundred fifty billion dollars (some expenditures are offset through tuition, endowment income, and so on), it is still vast. And even the gross total is meaningful as an index of the scale of national commitment. President Clinton refers to this sort of spending as an investment in human capital. If that is so, it seems reasonable to ask whether the investment pays a worthwhile rate of return. At its present size, the American style of mass higher education probably ought to be judged a mistake—and one based on a giant lie.

Why do people go to college? In an idealistic world, they might go to develop a capacity for critical thinking, enhance an already grounded knowledge of the sciences and world culture, learn further how to deal with other people's diversity of opinion and background, and in general become better citizens. They might go for fun, for friendship, for a network of contacts. They might go for spiritual enrichment or for pragmatic honing of skills.

In the real world, though, mostly they go to college to make money.

This reality is acknowledged in the mass media, which are forever running stories and charts showing how much a college degree contributes to lifetime income (with the more sophisticated publications very occasionally noting the counterweight costs of tuition paid and income foregone during the years of full-time study). These stories are no surprise to parents, who certainly wouldn't shell out the same money for travel or other exercises in fulfillment that do not result in a marketable credential. The income statistics are, similarly, no surprise to banks, which avidly market student loans and have been known to shower new graduates or even undergraduates with credit cards. And of course the stories are no surprise to students, who avidly follow news of where the jobs are and what starting salaries they command.

But the equation between college and wealth is not so simple. College graduates unquestionably do better on average economically than those who don't go at all. At the extremes, those with five or more years of college earn about triple the income of those with eight or fewer years of total schooling. Taking more typical examples, one finds that those who stop their educations after earning a four-year degree earn about one and a half times as much as those who stop at the end of high school. These outcomes, however, reflect other things besides the impact of the degree itself. College graduates are winners in part because colleges attract people who are already winners—people with enough brains and drive that they would do well in almost any generation and under almost any circumstances, with or without formal credentialing. The harder and more meaningful question is whether the mediocrities who have also flooded into colleges in the past couple of generations do better than they otherwise would have. And if they do, is it because college actually made them better employees or because it simply gave them the requisite credential to get interviewed and hired? Does having gone to college truly make one a better salesman of stocks or real estate or insurance? Does it enhance the work of a secretary or nanny or hairdresser? Does it make one more adept at running a car dealership or a catering company? Or being a messenger boy? All these occupations are being pursued, on more than an interim basis, by college graduates of my acquaintance. Most readers can probably think of parallel or equivalent examples. It need hardly be added that these occupations are also pursued, often with equal success, by people who didn't go to college at all, and in generations past were pursued primarily by people who hadn't stepped onto a campus. Indeed, the United States Labor Department's Bureau of Labor Statistics reported in 1994 that about twenty percent of all college graduates toil in fields not requiring a degree, and this total is projected to exceed thirty percent by the year 2005. For the individual, college may well be a credential without being a qualification, required without being requisite.

For American society, the big lie underlying higher education is akin to the aforementioned big lie about childrearing
in Garrison Keillor's Lake Wobegon: that everyone can be
above average. In the unexamined American Dream rhetoric
promoting mass higher education in the nation of my youth,
the implicit vision was that one day everyone, or at least practically everyone, would be a manager or a professional. We
would use the most elitist of all means, scholarship, toward the
most egalitarian of ends. We would all become chiefs; hardly
anyone would be left a mere Indian. On the surface this New
Jerusalem appears to have arrived. Where half a century ago
the bulk of jobs were blue collar, now a majority are white or
pink collar. They are performed in an office instead of on a
factory floor. If they still tend to involve repetition and drudg-
ery, at least they do not require heavy lifting.

But the wages for them are going down virtually as often as
up. It has become an axiom of union lobbying that replacing a
manufacturing economy with a service economy has meant
exporting once-lucrative jobs to places where they can be
done more cheaply. And as a great many disappointed office
workers have discovered, being better educated and better
dressed at the workplace does not transform one's place in the
pecking order. There are still plenty more Indians than chiefs.
Lately, indeed, the chiefs are becoming even fewer. If, for a
generation or so, corporate America bought into the daydream of making everyone a boss, the wakeup call has come.
The major focus of the "downsizing" of recent years has been
eliminating layers of middle management—much of it drawn
from the ranks of those lured to college a generation or two
ago by the idea that a degree would transform them from
mediocre to magisterial.

Yet our colleges blithely go on "educating" many more
prospective managers and professionals than we are likely to
need. In my own field, there are typically more students ma-
joring in journalism at any given moment than there are jour-

nalists employed at all the daily newspapers in the United States. A few years ago there were more students enrolled in law school than there were partners in all law firms. As trends shift, there have been periodic oversupplies of M.B.A.-wielding financial analysts, of grade school and high school teachers, of computer programmers, even of engineers. Inevitably many students of limited talent spend huge amounts of time and money pursuing some brass ring occupation, only to see their dreams denied. As a society we consider it cruel not to give them every chance at success. It may be more cruel to let them go on fooling themselves.

Just when it should seem clear that we are probably already doing too much to entice people into college, Bill Clinton is suggesting we do even more. In February 1994, for example, the President asserted that America needs a greater fusion between academic and vocational training—not because too many mediocre people misplaced on the college track are failing to acquire marketable vocational and technical skills, but because too many people on the vocational track are being denied courses that will secure them admission to college. Surely what we Americans need is not a fusion of the two tracks but a sharper division between them, coupled with a forceful program for diverting intellectual also-rans out of the academic track and into the vocational one. That is where most of them are heading in life anyway. Why should they wait until they are older and must enroll in high-priced proprietary vocational programs of often dubious efficacy—frequently throwing away not only their own funds but federal loans in the process—because they emerged from high school heading nowhere and knowing nothing that is useful in the marketplace?

If the massive numbers of college students reflected a national boom in love of learning and a prevalent yen for self-improvement, America's investment in the classroom might make sense. There are introspective qualities that can enrich any society in ways beyond the material. But one need look no further than the curricular wars to understand that most students are not looking to broaden their spiritual or intellectual horizons. They see themselves as consumers buying a product, and insist on applying egalitarian rules of the marketplace to what used to be an unchallenged elitism of the intellect.

Consider three basic trends, all of them implicit rejections of intellectual adventure, all based on seeing college in transactional terms. First, students are demanding courses that reflect and affirm their own identities in the most literal way. Rather than read a Greek dramatist of two thousand years ago and thrill to the discovery that some ideas and emotions are universal, many insist on reading writers of their own gender or ethnicity or sexual preference, ideally writers of the present or the recent past. They proclaim that they cannot (meaning, of course, *will* not) relate to heritages other than their own. Furthermore, they repudiate the idea that anyone can transcend his heritage—apparently because few if any people of their own heritage are judged to have done so, and they see the very idea of "universal values" in terms of some sort of competition that their group cannot win. This is parallel to the appalling trend in history, scathingly described in several recent essays by that brilliant traditionalist Gertrude Himmelfarb, in which all fact and analysis are dismissed as "relative" and theoretical opinion is enshrined as a liberating and morally superior form of scholarship. Historians have always known, she writes in *On Looking into the Abyss,* "what postmodernism professes to have just discovered"—that historical writing "is necessarily imperfect, tentative and partial." But previous generations did not embrace the drive to be "imaginative," "inventive," and "creative" rather than as truthful as circumstances permit.

Professors who pander to these students often talk in terms of liberation but they reject the most liberating of all intellectual undertakings, the journey beyond one's own place and time. For their part, many students do not want college to liberate or change them. They want it merely to reinforce them as they are, and they are in their way as unimaginative and smug as the white-bread fraternity dolts Sinclair Lewis so deftly sketched in *Elmer Gantry* and *Babbitt*. Often this self-absorption and lack of intellectual humility leads them to demand a curriculum that fails to serve even their base interests. At my own alma mater, Yale, undergraduates have been able to study Yoruba and other African tribal languages of extremely limited economic utility because these pursuits had sentimental or political appeal. But because there wasn't similar pressure for teaching Korean, they were denied the opportunity to enroll in a tongue that might actually have enabled them to get a job. San Francisco State has been offering a minor in gay studies for years, and organizations of professorial ideologues are pushing nationally for majors and even graduate degrees in the field. This may lead to a self-perpetuating career stream in academe. But what happens to an unsuspecting adolescent who minors in gay studies and then has to tell a job interviewer at, say, an insurance company that during the years when he might have been acquiring economically useful knowledge he was instead enrolled in such actual courses as Gay Male Relationships and Gays in Film? I'm not just worrying about the chilling effect of homophobia here. The same caveat applies to all ideologically based and impractical studies, like the feminist dialectics in the humanities that one female Columbia professor of my acquaintance dismisses as "clit lit," or Stanford's Black Hair as Culture and History. This sort of feel-good learning epitomizes the endemic confusion of the roles of the curriculum with those of the counseling service.

The second trend, implicit in the first, is that the curriculum has shifted from being what professors desire to teach to being what students desire to learn. In the heyday of faculty authority, professors devised set courses based on their view of the general basis for a liberal education, the essentials in each particular field, and, frequently, their personal intellectual interests. This system clearly served the professors (and nothing wrong with that), but it also served students by giving them teachers who were motivated, even excited, by the topics under discussion. My own college education took place during the Vietnam era, a time of abundance at most colleges because of government subsidy coupled with burgeoning enrollments due to the baby boom and draft avoidance. Professors could indulge their eccentricities; my freshman calculus teacher spent the entire fall term talking about his true love, Babylonian number theory, and I am probably the better for it, if only for a sense of the eons of continuity underlying all the great branches of scholarship.

Nowadays colleges have to hustle for students by truckling trendily. If the students want media studies programs so they can all fantasize about becoming TV news anchors, then media studies will abound, even though most real journalists have studied something substantive in college and that subset of TV news people who are mere personalities get by, of course, on charm and cheekbones rather than anything learned in a classroom. There are in any given year some three hundred thousand students enrolled in undergraduate communications courses. I know this because I was romanced heavily by a publishing house to write a textbook for this field. My interest dwindled when I learned that I should not expect to sustain any passage on a particular topic for even as much as a thousand words because these "future communicators" had short attention spans and didn't like to read. The idea of basing a text on what and how students *ought* to learn rather than on what and how they *wish* to learn apparently never enters the discussion. The market makes the rules, and control of the market has slipped from deservedly imperious professors to baselessly arrogant students. It is one thing to question authority, as the lapel buttons of my youth urged. It is quite another to ignore it altogether, as students often do today.

This shift of curricular power from teachers to students plainly affects what goes on in the classroom. I suspect it also affects scholarship for the worse. While one hopes that professors would use scholarly writing as an avenue for highbrow concerns that they find increasingly difficult to pursue within their courses, anecdotal evidence strongly suggests they don't. In reporting several stories for *Time* on the general topics of political correctness and multiculturalism, I discovered again and again that professors were instead writing to position themselves favorably on the ideological battlefield—or at least to exploit the marketplace for fulmination created by the culture wars.

Of even greater significance than the solipsism of students and the pusillanimity of teachers is the third trend, the sheer decline in the amount and quality of work expected in class. In an egalitarian environment the influx of mediocrities relentlessly lowers the general standard at colleges to the level the weak ones can meet. When my mother went to Trinity College in Washington in the early 1940s, at a time when it was regarded more as a finishing school for nice Catholic girls from the Northeast than as a temple of discipline, an English major there was expected to be conversant not only in English and Latin but also in Anglo-Saxon and medieval French. A course labeled "Carlisle, Ruskin, and Newman" meant, as my mother wearily recalled, "everything ever written by Carlisle, Ruskin, or Newman and also, it seemed, everything ever written *about* Carlisle, Ruskin, or Newman." A course in Shakespeare meant reading the plays, all thirty-seven of them. By the time I went to college, it was possible to get out of Yale as an honors English major without ever having read Chaucer or Spenser; I know, because I did. In today's indulgent climate, a professor friend at a fancy college told me as I was writing this chapter, taking a half semester of Shakespeare compels students to read exactly four plays. "Anything more than one a week," he explained, "is considered too heavy a load."

This probably should not be thought surprising in an era when most colleges, even prestigious ones, run some sort of remedial program for freshmen to learn the reading and writing skills they ought to have developed in junior high school —not to mention an era when many students vociferously object to being marked down for spelling or grammar. Indeed, all the media attention paid to curriculum battles at Stanford, Dartmouth, and the like obscures the even bleaker reality of American higher education. Or so argues Russell Jacoby, a sometime professor of history at various American and Canadian universities, in his compellingly cranky *Dogmatic Wisdom*. Most students, he notes, are enrolled at vastly less demanding institutions, where any substantial reading list, of whatever ethnicity, would be an improvement. Jacoby admiringly cites Clifford Adelman's *Tourists in Our Land*, based on a survey of the schooling of some twenty thousand high school students, most of them not elite. "When one looks at the archive left by an entire generation," he quotes Adelman as saying, "it should be rather obvious that Stanford is not where America goes to college. Whether Stanford freshmen read Cicero or Frantz Fanon is a matter worthy of a raree show." Well, not quite. For all its intermittent palaver about the individual, the academy is one of the national centers of copycat behavior and groupthink. If a Stanford professor makes a curricular choice, dozens if not hundreds of his would-be peers elsewhere will imitate that choice. Some of them daydream that by doing so they will one day actually teach at Stanford. Most of the rest fantasize that by aping Stanford and its ilk they make their vastly lesser institutions somehow part of the same echelon.

Perhaps it seems pettish to include community colleges and erstwhile state teachers' colleges when talking about the shortcomings of higher education. Most readers who went to more prestigious institutions think of "college" as meaning only their alma maters and the equivalents in cachet, and many expect (perhaps secretly even welcome) deficiencies at lesser places, because those failings reaffirm the hierarchy. But in terms of public expenditure, community colleges are probably much more expensive per capita for the taxpayer than any serious centers of learning, precisely because they tend to be relatively cheap for the student—and unlike private colleges, they rarely have significant endowments or other resources to offset the gap between the subsidized price and the true cost. Moreover, so long as these schools go on labeling themselves "colleges"—the word "junior" was widely dropped because it was demeaning, a perfect example of both euphemism and grade inflation—and so long as their students think of themselves as having "gone to college," their academic standards will color the public understanding of what college is.

When Vance Packard wrote *The Status Seekers* in the 1950s, he described the role of the better prep schools and colleges as grooming the next generation of the traditional ruling class while credentialing the ablest of those not quite to the manor born. The America he described was unprepared for the radicalism of college students in the 1960s. That political aggression was bred in part by Vietnam and the civil rights movement, but at least as much by social class anxieties among the burgeoning numbers of students whose parents had not gone to college and whose toehold on privilege was either shaky or nonexistent. The current college generation is similarly radical and dismissive of tradition for much the same reasons.

Those whose parents didn't go to college come disproportionately from ethnic minorities who are demanding a rewriting of the curriculum. This, not incidentally, is an effective means of leveling the playing field to their competitive advantage. If your classroom competitor possesses knowledge you don't, you better your prospects if you can get that knowledge declared irrelevant—and even more if you can get your homeboy hairstyle studied as culture and history.

Those whose parents did go to college are not necessarily any more confident. They have witnessed the economic erosion of the past couple of decades, in which it now takes two incomes for a family to live as well as it used to on one.

Both groups are understandably insistent on keeping the number of places in college as large as possible, for fear of having to drop their dreams. This form of middle-class welfare (even college students not raised in the middle class are by definition seeking to enter it) is shamelessly indulged by state legislators who recognize it as a necessity for reelection.

Other constituencies join in pushing for the maintenance and expansion of public higher education. Faculty and administrators seek to protect their jobs. Merchants and civic boosters serve their interests, both economic and sentimental, by bolstering institutions that bear the name of their town or state. Alumni often combine a nostalgic loyalty with a pragmatic one. They think, with some justice, that burnishing the luster of their alma mater adds to the sheen of their own education as well, even though it was acquired years or decades ago and has nothing to do with the merits or deficiencies of the institution of today.

But none of these social pressures justifies spending one hundred fifty billion dollars a year overeducating a populace that is neither consistently eager for intellectual expansion of horizons nor consistently likely to gain the economic and professional status for which the education is undertaken. Nor can one justify such expenditures by citing the racial and ethnic pressures from those who argue that only a wide-open system of higher education will give minorities a sufficient chance. Whatever the legacy of discrimination or the inadequacies of big-city high schools, a C student is a C student and turning colleges into remedial institutions for C students (or worse) only debases the value of the degrees the schools confer.

Beyond the material cost of college, there are other social costs implicit in our system of mass higher education. If college is not difficult to get into, students are not as likely to be motivated in high school. If the authority of a teacher's grade or recommendation is not vital because there will always be a place open at some college somewhere, students have yet another reason for disrespecting authority and learning less efficiently. Paying for their children's college education often imposes a massive financial drain on parents during the years when they should be most intent on preparing for retirement, and leaves many of them too dependent on Social Security and other welfare programs. (Any reader who has not yet grasped that Social Security is not an insurance program but is instead, and always has been, a wealth transfer between generations will want to pay especially close attention to Chapter Eight.) This expenditure may make sense when the education has real value for the child being supported. But some parents are wasting their money.

For many adolescents who finish high school without a clear sense of direction, college is simply a holding pattern until they get on with their lives. It is understandable that they should want to extend their youth and ponder their identities (or navels) for a bit; what is rather less clear is why they should do so at public as well as parental expense. At minimum, that opportunity ought to be limited to students who have shown some predisposition to absorb a bit of learning while they are waiting to discover their identities.

My modest proposal is this. Let us reduce, over perhaps a five-year span, the number of high school graduates who go on to college from nearly sixty percent to a still generous thirty-three percent. This will mean closing a lot of institutions. Most of them, in my view, should be community colleges, current or former state teachers' colleges, and the like.

These schools serve the academically marginal and would be better replaced by vocational training in high school and on-the-job training at work. Two standards should apply in judging which schools to shut down. First, what is the general academic level attained by the student body? That might be assessed in a rough and ready way by requiring any institution wishing to survive to give a standardized test—say, the Graduate Record Examination—to all its seniors. Those schools whose students perform below the state norm would face cutbacks or closing. Second, what community is being served? A school that serves a high percentage of disadvantaged students (this ought to be measured by family finances rather than just race or ethnicity) can make a better case for receiving tax dollars than one that subsidizes the children of the prosperous, who have private alternatives. Even ardent egalitarians should recognize the injustice of taxing people who wash dishes or mop floors for a living to pay for the below-cost public higher education of the children of lawyers, so that they can go on to become lawyers too.

This reduction would have several salutary effects. The public cost of education would be sharply reduced. Competitive pressures would probably make high school students and their schools perform better. Businesses, which now depend on colleges to make their prospective employees at least minimally functional, would foot some of the bills—and doubtless would start demanding that high schools fulfill their duty of turning out literate, competent graduates. And, of course, those who devise college curricula might get the message that skills and analytical thinking are the foremost objects of learning—not sociopolitical self-fulfillment and ideological attitudinizing.

I would like to preserve, however, one of the few indisputably healthy trends in higher education, the opening up of the system to so-called mature students (meaning, in practice, mostly housewives). Here is where open admission makes sense. Anyone who has been out of high school for, say, seven or perhaps ten years ought to be allowed to enroll and perhaps even be offered the chance to purchase a semester of not-for-credit refresher courses. If people of that age are prepared to make the sacrifices and undertake the disciplines of being students again, they are likely to succeed—indeed, at most schools that actively solicit mature students, the older enrollees outperform the younger ones.

Massive cuts in total college enrollment would, of course, necessitate massive layoffs of faculty. In my educational utopia, that would be the moment to eliminate tenure and replace it with contracts of no more than five years, after which renewal should be possible but not presumed. This would allow universities to do some of the same weeding out of underproductive managers and professionals that has made American business more efficient, and would compel crackpot ideologues of whatever stripe to justify their scholarship, at least to their peers and conceivably to the broader public. The justification normally offered for tenure—the potential for a revival of McCarthyism—is so remote from present-day academic reality as not to be worthy of discussion. And just what is wrong with having to defend one's opinion anyway? A college teaching position is an opportunity to think and serve, not a professor's personal capital asset. Apart from the self-interest of professors, it is hard to concoct any other rationale for affording college teachers a tenure protection enjoyed by few other managers and professionals, save civil servants who operate under much closer supervision and scrutiny. Competing for one's job on an ongoing basis could introduce a little more healthy elitism into the professorial lifestyle. Teachers might strive to meet standards more widely held than their own ideology. The risk is that the loss of tenure could make professors even more apt to kowtow to the consumerist demands of students, so as to remain popular and employed. But that is happening anyway.

In truth, I don't expect any suggestion as sweeping as mine

to be enacted. America is in the grip of an egalitarianism so pervasive that low grades are automatically assumed to be the failure of the school and the teacher and perhaps the community at large—anyone but the student himself. We insist on saying that pretty much everyone can learn, that it's only a matter of tapping untouched potential. While we are ready to call someone handicapped "differently abled," we are not ready to label the dull-witted as "differently smart." Even more than in my youth, we cling to the dream of a world in which everyone will be educated, affluent, technically adept, his or her own boss. There is nothing wrong with discontent at having a modest place in the scheme of things. That very discontent produced the ambition that built the culture of yesterday and today. But the discontent of those times was accompanied by discipline, willingness to work hard, and ready acceptance of a competitive society.

Some readers may find it paradoxical that a book arguing for greater literacy and intellectual discipline should lead to a call for less rather than more education. Even if college students do not learn all they should, the readers' counterargument would go, surely they learn something, and that is better than their learning nothing. Maybe it is. But at what price? One hundred fifty billion dollars is awfully high for deferring the day when the idle or ungifted take individual responsibility and face up to their fate. And the price is even steeper when the egalitarian urge has turned our universities, once museums of clear ideas, into soapboxes for hazy and tribalist ones. Ultimately it is the yearning to believe that anyone can be brought up to college level that has brought colleges down to everyone's level.

SEVEN

Noah's Ark,
Feminist Red Riding Hood,
Karaoke Peasants,
and the Joy of Cooking

Dear Michael,

As *The Paris Review* enters its fortieth year, we wish to thank the literary agents and friends of the magazine who have brought us many of the stories, essays and poems that we have published over the years. You, and the authors to whom you have introduced us, have enabled *The Paris Review* to keep its standards high.

In preparation for *The Paris Review*'s fortieth anniversary issue, scheduled for the fall of 1993, we ask you to outdo yourselves in our behalf yet again. The issue will be a fat one, outstanding in content as well as heft. To that end, I hope you will keep an eye out for the very best work by your strongest writers. We are also particularly keen to see worthy pieces by women and minority writers. . . .

Yours sincerely,
George Plimpton,
Editor

—Actual letter to my agent, dated October 30, 1992

THE LETTER QUOTED on the previous page startled me the first time I read it and it startles me still, chiefly because it seems not to have startled anyone else. The quota-mindedness it reveals is jarring enough. What is truly stunning is the degree of desensitization throughout our intellectual culture that allows an editor to express his values so baldly and the mailing's recipients to absorb it without apparent public fuss. Surely, even in this day and age, it should strike someone as preposterous for a man to pose as a defender of "standards" and then, in the next breath, acknowledge that his standards are blatantly dual—demanding "the very best work" from white men yet settling for the merely "worthy" from people of more fashionable race and sex. Given the snooty history and relative cachet of *The Paris Review,* there if anywhere one ought to find uncompromising insistence on quality and consistency. Instead, in every corner of American culture from the august to the obscure, art is busily being subordinated to politics.

Fairy tales are rewritten to make them more suitably feminist and nonviolent. The new Little Golden Sound series takes much of the scare out of *The Three Little Pigs* and *Chicken Little,* which seems to nullify the point of these cautionary tales about prudence. Little Golden's new version of *Little Red Riding Hood* eliminates not only the wolf's eating of the heroine and her grandmother but also the whole character of the woodsman who comes to their rescue by slitting open the beast's belly. The original is judged much too gory and not nice enough to the predator to satisfy animal rights activists. Above all, women aren't supposed to have to depend on men to rescue them, not even if they are young and inexperienced or old and frail. So in the rewritten tale, the wolf chases Grandma into a closet, where she hides until Red Riding Hood comes. Then Grandma jumps out and scares the wolf away by wearing a ghost costume (!) as the ladies savor their empowerment.

Stage plays such as David Mamet's *Oleanna* are condemned by critics not for failings of narrative or stagecraft, but for taking the "wrong" side on such issues as sexual harassment. Mamet suggests in his play that some charges of harassment result from misunderstanding and some may be altogether baseless. In many instances, he implies, what is labeled sexual is really a dispute over power. In a key passage, the accusatory student tells her professor that he is unforgivably "elitist" for teaching what he thinks students should learn rather than polling them for their demands of what they want to know. Hardly any reviews either in New York or in London forebore to take sides on the political issue, and reviewers seemed to forget that Mamet was attempting a work of art rather than a piece of journalism. Much the same fate befell Michael Crichton's previously cited novel *Disclosure,* which centers on a male executive's claim of sexual harassment against a female superior. Reviewers widely felt obliged to point out that this was unrepresentative of the "real problem," both to demonstrate their feminist political credentials and to establish that art must always be litmus-tested for its ideological propriety.

In universities these days, many classic novels are viewed with suspicion because they do not have gay or feminist characters. Never mind that such thinking was unknown or at least repressed in the authors' time. The obligation of art to parallel life applies only when life is politically correct. (In Britain, an elementary school principal took this revisionism to the extreme in early 1994 when she declined an offer of free tickets for her pupils to attend a ballet version of *Romeo and Juliet.*

Her objection: The story is "blatantly heterosexual" and, like most classics, does not sufficiently acquaint students with alternative family structures and lifestyles. When it emerged a couple of days later that the principal was living with the woman who chaired the school board that hired her, the story dominated London headlines—even crowding out the supermarket clerk who successfully demanded that her chain rename gingerbread men "gingerbread persons.")

Shakespeare actually did write some apparently gay characters but is widely taught as having been "racist" and "sexist" because he reflects some social assumptions of his time—and because of his iconic significance. As Paul Kantor, a University of Virginia professor, has so compellingly argued in *The Public Interest*, "To uncover the biases in Shakespeare becomes a way of uncovering the narrowmindedness and exclusivity of Western culture, and thus in turn a way of pursuing the agenda of many members of the contemporary academy . . . the obsession with identity politics."

American Theater, an ostensibly objective magazine that in fact assumes, as so many current intellectual journals do, that all virtue is to be found in the identity-politics left, demands in a March 1994 cover headline, "Why Don't We See More Plays by Black Women?" It does not ask why we don't see more *good* plays by black women; it proceeds on the certitude that if such works are not being staged, the reasons have nothing to do with inherent value. The focal subject of the article, Suzan-Lori Parks, told *The New York Times* in a contemporaneous interview that one of her favorite writers is Samuel Beckett because, she said, "He just seems so black to me." Heaven forfend that she acknowledge that his art is universal and that its clarity transcends time, place, gender, and color. No, if she relates to him, it must be because of his imaginary "blackness."

Even awards that are ostensibly meant to honor the best intellectual and creative work are often tainted by concerns of identity politics. Toni Morrison's Pulitzer Prize in fiction for *Beloved* came after an explicitly race-based lobbying campaign on her behalf, with a modicum of feminist pressure thrown in as well. August Wilson is probably the foremost American dramatist of our day and he has been a Pulitzer Prize finalist for at least three plays, winning twice. But the first time he won, the Pulitzer board was attracted above all to the idea that he was a black high school dropout and therefore overturned a drama jury of professional critics who favored another play. Board members said privately that they wanted to send a message of hope to black America—admirable, but hardly reflecting the purpose of the award.

The National Book Awards, according to people much involved in their administration, have become a beehive of identity tokenism. Judges have been chosen because they are likely to vote for blacks or Hispanics or women. This aim, explicitly acknowledged in private sessions, has been accompanied by rhetoric about "exploitation" and what the exploited groups deserve in recompense. "Diversity" was the buzzword when the nonfiction award went to Paul Monette's gay and AIDS memoir *On Becoming a Man*—a book that I admire but that some of the people who honored it reportedly did not regard as the best of its year. One disgruntled former Book Awards official says, "The political-correctness people fight as dirty as the capitalists ever did. I didn't go public. This was one of the few fights in my life I ever backed off from, because I couldn't win. When I asked why we chose judges only from among left-wing academics instead of working writers, there was definitely discussion that the writers could not be counted on to vote a certain way. They were too independent."

The emphasis on tribalism, tokenism, and toeing the political line is, if anything, more painful in the realm of culture, which traditionally represents the highest aspirations of the individual, than it is in other realms of the life of the mind.

But it is, appallingly, by no means the worst manifestation of run-amok egalitarianism in the arts and media. Just as troubling are the decline in respect for technique and skill (except, perhaps, on the basketball court); the equation of what is popular with what is good; the free rein given in scholarship, entertainment, and even journalism to magic, mysticism, miracles, mind-reading, and other alleged manifestations of the supernatural; the dumbing-down of journalism; and the emergence of a series of entertainment forms and home technologies that foster the tireless self-celebration of the peasantry for the mere fact of being alive. Not least, there is the emergence of the music video, in which linear thinking gives way to sensory (and sensual) imagery, sans connection, sans analysis, sans narrative or moral. Combine this esthetic (or lack thereof) with a computer and what comes next is "virtual reality," an even more absorbingly sensory ego trip for the masses, no longer in pursuit of instruction or the contemplation of beauty but simply in search of self. Along that path may lie egalitarianism's final victory. Elitists cannot be elite without disciples. As mass pop culture increasingly gives way to private narcissism, even the oblique and refracted elitism of those who influence pop culture from afar may simply wither away.

The very phrase "American culture" has been a standing subject of mockery by Eurocentrists who found the art of our erstwhile colony too vulgar, too effusive, too explicit, and too rustic. What, they demanded rhetorically, was one to make of a people whose principal novels were about a boy on a raft and a man on a whaling ship, apart from the institutions and relationships of an urban society, and whose foremost films concerned a family of gangsters and a media mogul cum mountebank? How could one esteem a people whose principal musical expressions were songs, simple in form and a few minutes in length, and whose primary contributions to painting were reductivist abstractions largely devoid of historical reference and encoded language? When universities began inserting significant swatches of American culture into their humanities curricula, little more than half a century ago, it was an act of patriotic defiance more than of true esthetic confidence.

The logical next step in academic thinking began about a quarter century ago: emphasizing popular culture, in which the United States came to dominate world sensibilities, in preference to the classical culture in which Americans were chronologically doomed to be also-rans. That academic shift coincided with the rise of the National Endowment for the Arts and the National Endowment for the Humanities, and doubtless contributed to a populist emphasis in much of the grant-giving, an impulse initially dictated by pork barrel politics. By honoring quilt weavers and opera companies, folk festivals and Shakespeare festivals out of the same pot, the Endowment for the Arts effectively implied that these are comparable activities, of equivalent merit, and that the only choice to be made between them is one of personal taste and preference. This miscomprehension has not been so widespread inside the arts communities, in part because the Endowment maintained a system of peer review that was as much meritocratic as political. The public, however, could not be expected to be so discerning.

The idea that all cultural expressions are equal has been fostered, not surprisingly, by women and minorities. Just as Americans in general have felt more confident in their grasp of contemporary culture than of its classical antecedents predating our nationhood, so those Americans who were historically excluded from the mainstream of tastemaking now feel more comfortable with seeing their traditional crafts and pursuits elevated to the status of art than they do with trying to master established art forms. In truth, some of these crafts have much to recommend them. I collect vintage examples of weaving; I find the blues irresistible; I have always liked square dancing. But these are lesser forms of art than, say, oil painting and opera and ballet, because the techniques are less arduous and less demanding of long learning, the underlying symbolic language is less complicated, the range of expression is less profound, and the worship of beauty is muddied by the lower aims of community fellowship. Above all, these arts are less intellectual—less cerebral, less abstract, less of a test. The prevailing popular notion that high culture is hard brain-work is, in fact, true. That is part of its point, not necessarily to exclude the less able but certainly to challenge them to stretch themselves and to heighten their learning.

American popular culture does not embrace this certification of art as work. Indeed, the word *art* is rarely used at all. The preferred signifier is the word *entertainment,* which correctly conveys that the aspirations are generally escapist, nostalgic, or anodyne. Entertainment promises to make you feel better, to help you forget your troubles, to liberate you from having to think. Even when entertainment touches deep feelings, it does so as a gesture of reassurance, a combination of sentiment and sloganeering. This is what most people say they want, and the market lets them have it, without anyone in a position of intellectual or social leadership telling them that they should ask more of themselves—and might benefit thereby.

This should not be taken as a blanket condemnation of Hollywood film, or even of network television. For the discerning—and the preternaturally patient—there is much on television, even commercial network television, that offers the complexity and challenge of art. There is more that is witty and occasionally provocative. But there is a glut of the stupid, the banal, and the coarse. And although the American people are ostensibly better educated, better read, and more worldly than when television was in its infancy and Hollywood in its populist heyday, both art forms now offer more chaff and less grain than they did forty years ago. There is no commercial television equivalent to *Playhouse 90* or *Studio One* or any of the several showcases for ambitious writing and acting in those days. *All About Eve* would not be made now, at least not with that literate and zinging script, and neither would *Come Back, Little Sheba* or *The Rose Tattoo* or even, probably, *Marty,* to cite a few Oscar winners of that time. The difference in what is considered viable is in part the result of the boom in potential profit, which has prompted producers always to go for the least common denominator, and in part the by-product of erosion in the general public will to recognize one's betters and try to emulate them, to know one's own deficiencies and seek to correct them, to sense one's ignorance and long to amend it.

The dominant mood of contemporary American culture is the self-celebration of the peasantry. I recognize the towering snobbery of that remark, especially by today's egalitarian standards, and I do not apologize for it. I believe I am talking about something deeper than the question of whether other people like what I like and, if not, whether they have a right to prefer their own taste. I think I am talking about values that inspire a society and make it cohere.

If you walk into the home of the average American, you will find the walls, tabletops, desks, and other flat surfaces crowded with works of art. You will find more such works of art in portfolios that are tucked away but frequently brought out for display to visitors. These works of art are usually the homeowner's most treasured possessions. During the Los Angeles fires of 1993, for example, the majority of people who were interviewed about their flight to safety said these artworks were the things they moved first to protect.

The artworks in question are, of course, photographs. Some have esthetic merit because of their composition. Some have the inherent merit of depicting beautiful places, albeit usually in a cramped and color-errant rendition. Most are simply documents approximating where people were and how they looked on some particular day, a day perhaps memorable only to the participants and often not memorable even to them. Ceremonies such as weddings rate dozens if not hundreds of pictures. Christmases and birthdays get almost equally exhaustive treatment. While fashion has happily changed to spare us the Victorian penchant for portraits of stillborn babies and toddlers who died young, living relatives are honored in abundance, often on the apparent principle that more photographs per person is proof of more love. These laboriously assembled pictures usually represent a large expenditure of money and, even more, of time. It has become a commonplace observation that getting the photograph right often seems more important than the actual experience it records. Displaying these photos has become the primary decorating statement in many households (there are still a few where tinted pictures of the bleeding heart of Jesus are more prominent, just as there are many teenagers' rooms where posters of rock stars, sports figures, or women in swimsuits take precedence).

This custom might be regarded as innocuous were it not for what is crowded off the walls and desktops. What is supplanted is art chosen for its beauty, for its representation of some esthetic ideal to be aspired to, and also art chosen for its instructive quality as a depiction of some person or type to be emulated, that is, some hero for our antiheroic and mistrustful age. The family photograph is, instead, art chosen for comfort, the domestic equivalent of entertainment.

The underlying statement in accumulating and displaying family photographs is that the life of the family, obsessively recorded but not analyzed or contextualized, is the most important thing in the world, at least to those who live under that particular roof. The existence being celebrated is deemed praiseworthy merely for the fact of taking place. Rituals of accomplishment—graduation from high school or college, sporting victories, and the like—are at best treated no more grandly than rituals of emotional renewal, such as family re-unions. The prevalent political rhetoric about "family values," heard mostly from the right but increasingly from the Democratic left as well, is an attempt to tap into the clan smugness of the picture-takers. When Americans are told over and over that family is the most important thing in life, what they hear is not a message of mutual responsibility and ambition. They hear that their lives rank as rich and accomplished merely by virtue of their having survived and reproduced and put food on the table, and they ask no more of themselves.

The cheap home camera is of course an old invention by now. So is the Polaroid, with its instant development, instant gratification, instant turning of an ephemeral event into one worthy of preservation. Home movies are technologically passé as well. Now it is the age of the camcorder, which seductively combines the instantaneousness of the Polaroid with the ego boost of being able to see oneself on television, the medium that also reports news of achievement—so that one can unconsciously feel one has demonstrated the epochal value of a backyard spaghetti fest. About the only thing one can say in favor of the camcorder is that it includes a sound feature. Most of what people say into its microphone is so inane and stupefyingly dull, even to them, that they cannot bear to watch the tapes played back very often.

This harrumph against the chronicling of the everyday does not mean that great art never arises from ordinary lives. People do not come much more ordinary than the Lomans in *Death of a Salesman* or the Wingfields in *The Glass Menagerie*. What makes those works important is not the banal events and rela-tionships being chronicled but the clear-eyed, deep-digging analytical thought and emotional perception of the writer. The ordinariness of the lives portrayed may contribute to the breadth of a work's outreach. The crucial factor is the depth of its insight. The same is true in other forms—Edward Hop-

per's paintings of diners, Diane Arbus's photographs of unpre-
possessing families, John Steinbeck's *The Grapes of Wrath* and
its many adaptations. Art that settles for mere identification—
for the feeling of seeing oneself, as in a mirror—is of not
much greater value than those piles of Polaroids from family
reunions and those tedious videotapes of Baby Jane.

But the celebration of normalcy is not limited to this
household clutter. Popular culture is full of manifestations of
the implicit, and sometimes even explicit, idea that to be average is to be ideal. Stand-up comics, whose presence is proliferating on television and in night spots, typically base more
than half of their routines on references to other television
images and catch phrases, particularly from commercials.
These allusions win surefire laughs from audiences, not because of any display of wit or insight, but because the audience
has the comfort of recognition, of knowing it's on familiar
turf and clued in to the gag. Or consider that paradigm of
entertainment intersecting with pseudo-instruction, the game
show. There is only one *Jeopardy!*—only one show where
there are identifiable right and wrong responses and where
having paid attention in the classroom will actually do you
some good. The vastly more common model is *Family Feud,*
where the goal is to guess the answer (to always broad, sometimes vague, and mostly inane questions) given most often by
other Americans in a poll. The point is not to be right or
knowledgeable but simply to resemble the norm. If other
people think cheese is a vegetable or Paris a country, then you
will be better off thinking so too, however much of an ignora-
mus that makes you. The device of guessing other people's
responses in order to win underlies most game shows. The
bulk of the rest depend, like *Wheel of Fortune,* on gambling
and the lottery mentality decried in the opening chapter.
While some *Wheel* contestants keep spinning because they are
benighted numbskulls (like the woman I saw confronted with
"Secretar_ _f State Ge_rge Sh_ _t_" who said, "Give me an

M, please"), most know the answer long before they solve the puzzle and keep going in hope of racking up more money. The game's drama comes from risk, not brains. Its final segment has been made much easier, with forty percent of the letters in the alphabet revealed in each puzzle, so that both players and viewers at home can be right more often. People watch game shows to play along, and they want to congratulate themselves on their acuity; the games keep being simplified until nearly everyone can call himself a winner.

In a society that seems to have lost its capacity for admiration, we have shifted from having heroes to having entertainers or celebrities (the distinction between the latter two may not always be clear, but my rule of thumb is that an entertainer is someone who can actually do something, someone who has a verifiable skill or talent, whereas Vanna White is a celebrity). The place of the entertainer at the center of national consciousness cannot be overstated. Norman Schwarzkopf may have had his day in the sun, but it soon ended. By contrast, everything to do with basketball player Michael Jordan, from his golf bets to his relatives, is obsessive national news. The disappearance and murder of Jordan's father made headlines for weeks; on the day, soon after the murder, when Jordan retired from the game, NBC anchored its nightly newscast from where Jordan spoke; and Jordan's attempts to switch to professional baseball attracted only slightly less notice than the dismembering of Sarajevo. The preoccupation with entertainers at the expense of politicians, generals, and statesmen is not just a sign of cynicism, although there is plenty of that about. It is also a measure of how society has changed. Where once Americans cheered for people who represented character traits they would like to embody and who had achieved greatness they would like to rival, we now cheer mainly for people who amuse us. Being entertained is plainly a shallower pursuit than being inspired. Moreover, it is a self-absorbed and inward-looking one, a pursuit centered on the personal and, usually, the passive side of life rather than on the worldly and the epic.

Even within the realm of entertainment, Americans are more apt than ever to admire the celebrated for their fame and money rather than for their technique and admittedly often minimal talent. Daydreams that one might become a star, too, are ever more plausible when stardom seems unconnected to innate gifts and long, hard work. This attitude appears to underlie the karaoke fad, which I found intensely irksome at its height. The idea, for anyone who may have been spared witnessing it in the flesh, is that one takes a microphone in a bar (where, if one is lucky, everyone in the audience is very drunk) and sings a pop hit while a machine plays the backup sound track sans the original lead vocalist. There isn't much room for real creativity; if one varies by more than a nanosecond from the precise phrasing and timing of the original, one falls hopelessly out of synch with the canned accompaniment. But the implicit message is that you, I, or indeed almost anyone can be a pop star, provided he has the proper accoutrements. I never imagined myself leaping to the defense of pop stars as models of cultivated craftsmanship; to me, music ended with Schubert. But it is ludicrous to suggest that the achievements of pop entertainers are purely a product of fortuitous fate and technological help, or that the world is awash in undiscovered talents loitering in bars, or for that matter that imitating a pop star syllable for syllable and breath for breath is anything more than the sincerest form of flattery. At its core, karaoke is not just a party trick but another egalitarian assertion that everyone is equal, or can be. In truth, some people are more talented than others, some more beautiful, some more interesting as personalities. Some people are born to be stars. Some are born to sit in the audience and applaud their betters.

Even more narcissistic than karaoke is the couch potatohood of watching music videos, the principal cultural

referent of the contemporary young. Like the music they focus on, videos make words subsidiary to images and sounds,
which means they retreat from the common ground of shared
experience to the personal dreamscape of individual viewers
who find their own meaning or at least feeling in each
vignette. Words do not, of course, mean exactly the same
thing to each person who uses them. But there is enough
discipline in the English language to ensure that the variations
are small. A person who displaces language for reverie has
every likelihood of finding both sense and sensation widely at
variance from what fellow viewers derive, or what the creators
intend.

Montage is a lazy artist's form, lacking a moral compass and
explicitly inviting individual audience members to find their
own interpretation and values rather than engage the artist's
passion and advocacy. That can work if one's audiences are
thoughtful art museum habitués. It is reckless abandonment
when the audience is callow youth. A few years ago I went
back to my old public high school to give a speech. When I
encouraged the audience of the suburban and prosperous
young to be more critical consumers of mass media, to try to
understand what messages they were deriving, they sat in
bored silence and looked at me as though I had two heads.
The only thing that woke them up was when I handed back
the check for my fee to be put in the school's scholarship
fund. This occurred before MTV took its death grip on the
young. The baffled indifference would be worse nowadays.

I do not mean to condemn a symptom as a cause. According to a United States Department of Education survey of
more than twenty-six thousand adult Americans, studied in
1992 and with data released in September 1993, a projected
fifteen million adults are entirely illiterate and another seventy-five million have only minimal reading and computation
skills. Some twenty-five million max out at being able to add
up the items on a bank deposit slip; another fifty million can

handle the subtraction needed in comparing the prices of two items but can't identify an error on a credit card bill and draft a coherent letter explaining what's wrong. In a nation where functional illiteracy or its moral equivalent is so widespread, the advent of music videos is at worst an exacerbation of a problem, not its trigger. But a style of communication that is deliberately nonlinear and nonnarrative, and that is usually unconcerned with logic, certainly won't enhance analytic acuity. Like so much else in popular culture, music videos may give the public what it wants, but they do almost nothing about giving the public what it needs.

The mass media and the entertainment-crazed society they foster have done artists an enormous favor in making their work seem more central to the human experience than ever before and in allowing so many of them to make a living, often an imperial one. Unsurprisingly, given the essential ingratitude of almost anyone with an ego big enough to be an artist—to say, in effect, "Look at me, because I am more interesting than you are"—the beneficiaries of this change are frequently less than thankful. They focus instead on the media appetite for vulgarity and easy accessibility and on the hype that substitutes for scholarship. They complain that whole styles of work get no attention because they are out of fashion and that the artists most revered by other artists are typically all but unknown to the general public. There is, of course, a touching naïveté in their not recognizing that if these darlings of the cognoscenti were more successful and richer, their peers might find it harder to admire them so much. In an October 1992 essay in *The New Republic* decrying the state of affairs, Jed Perl (an art critic married to a painter) asked, "Can artists keep on doing their damnedest when the wide world doesn't give a damn?" One would think that the life of Van Gogh, who sold exactly one painting while he was still around to enjoy the proceeds, settles this question forever in the affirmative. Perl argues that things are much tougher now; so, of course, does almost any writer, on any topic, when trying to work up sympathy for those he sees as ill used or downtrodden. Many artists of great talent find a popular following only in old age or death, as the innovative vigor of what they do becomes more easily comprehensible to the masses. But artists need to recognize that if they do not create for audiences, if they do not create to be understood, then what they are doing is not art—it is therapy.

It is probably impermissible to discuss American culture at any length without addressing Jesse Helms and the assault on the National Endowment for the Arts. While I personally prefer not to offer wall space in my home to photographs of a man with a whip up his butt, I share the general distaste for Helms's attempts to impose orthodoxy. His goal is, I think, misunderstood. His real target is not culture but homosexuality, the bugbear du jour of the paranoid right. The essence of Helms's argument is identical to the argument of the politically correct leftists whom he professes to view with such disdain: that there is a constitutional right not to be offended, not to have one's views challenged, not to be exposed to alien ideas. This, too, is egalitarian excess of a sort. It is a rejection of the marketplace of ideas, a refusal to believe that good thinking will prevail over fuzzy thinking. In Helms's case, the argument is that the proper poles of thought are good versus bad morally, not good versus fuzzy intellectually, and that the right way of thinking is divinely revealed and not subject to human debate. Helms may not share much ideologically with the politically correct, but he shares their intellectual insecurity and apparent emotional fragility. Only a fearful man insists that freedom of speech is less sacred than freedom *from* speech.

A few years ago the news director of the CBS-owned television station in New York City, the flagship of the network's affiliates, auditioned me to be a part-time on-air media critic.

(I didn't get the job.) In instructing me on what sort of sample pieces to prepare and how to phrase them, he told me to bear in my mind that my audience would be "ignorant housewives who learn what little they know about the world from television." At about the same time, Van Gordon Sauter, then president of CBS News and probably the brightest man ever to hold that job, said he had given up on the idea of expanding network news to an hour, due to affiliate resistance and lack of audience interest. In fact, he said, he was deliberately softening the half hour (in reality, twenty-two minutes plus commercials, promos, and chitchat) to include less hard news scrutinizing government and more human interest stories from around the world, ideally ending with some warm and fuzzy postcard item to cap each broadcast. A few years later, the New York affiliate station moved that network newscast, no longer overseen by Sauter, to a time slot half an hour earlier. This move had the network's permission, though CBS officials knew full well that it would doom the newscast to an audience made up of fewer job-holding professionals and more "ignorant housewives." They consoled themselves with the fact that *Entertainment Tonight*, which was moving to the half-hour slot following the news, would bring in more revenue and improve the already hugely profitable station's bottom line.

These actions by CBS may be deplorable, but they are hardly atypical. Both NBC and ABC have moved their newscasts earlier in New York City. Both of them have cut back massively on foreign bureaus and now pick up videotape from independent, often unsupervised news services that may depart from the networks' already lax standards of ethics. When it comes to pandering in pursuit of ratings, there is not much to choose among Connie Chung's copious CBS interviewing of unscrupulous skater Tonya Harding, Stone Phillips' NBC profile of mass murderer and cannibal Jeffrey Dahmer, or NBC's installation of rocketry into a supposedly defective truck to provoke splashy pictures of an explosion. Individual journalists, even broadcast journalists, may still claim to be committed to a higher calling. Dan Rather of CBS professes to be uninterested in commanding top ratings, and in a March 1994 letter to *The New York Times* he indignantly distinguished between news and its tabloid competitors such as *Hard Copy,* which he termed "news-influenced entertainment." But whatever such veterans as Rather may believe their role is, their paymasters are unflinchingly dedicated to profit. Print journalism is only marginally better, with *The New York Times* fattening its food and home furnishings coverage and many other newspapers exhaustively covering a boy's assertions about being shown Michael Jackson's allegedly speckled penis. This diving into the dirt is not simply an expression of capitalist greed. It reflects the abandonment of the high ground of elitism, of presuming to teach and improve the public, for the swamp of egalitarianism. In the egalitarian formulation, the definition of news is what the public wants to hear about or is already talking about. By this definition, the severing of John Wayne Bobbitt's penis is news, nonentity though he may be, while the needless swelling of the Pentagon budget is not. Giving the public what it wants, while trying to maximize one's audience, inevitably means concentrating on stories simple enough for the dumbest and most disinterested reader or listener to comprehend. That is the appeal of the Bobbitt story, the exploding truck story, the Tonya Harding story—each of them features a violent central act, fully within the range of understanding of a five-year-old.

Not all of the blame belongs to journalists. They are responding to the society in which they find themselves, a society where it is no longer considered a duty of citizenship to read a daily newspaper and try to grasp what is going on, a society in which the sacred right to vote is now exercised by only about half of those eligible to do so. Newspaper readership per household has dropped from an average of 1.3 dailies in the late 1940s to an average of two thirds of a daily today, or precisely half the peak level. The number of households getting a daily newspaper is in fact less than two thirds; some households, obviously, get two or more. Among those under thirty, the newspaper habit is rare indeed. Newspapers have been increasingly preoccupied for the past two decades with finding ways to reach that younger audience, but the problem has only grown worse. Hipness of tone, expansion of coverage, and hiring of the very young has done little to help, even when great newspapers went to such extremes as the Sunday "Styles of the Times" funkiness in *The New York Times* or the cultural coverage of *The Boston Globe,* which on some days runs more about rock and pop music than about all the other arts combined, in one of the few cities with a truly copious classical arts scene. The only news that seems to appeal to the young is MTV's, which emphasizes sermonettes about racism and condom use and which explained the violence in Sarajevo by (I'm not kidding) running a piece about how hard it was to make rock videos in the middle of a civil war. The continued pursuit of the young and the stupid is apt to lead to equally silly stories elsewhere. Chasing after an audience that does not want to be an audience for news can only speed the decline. Offering "news you can use," frequently sold with precisely that phrase, can only validate the shallow in their own torpor and ignorance. What America needs is a renewed reverence for fact, for knowledge, for citizen awareness.

What it does not need but is seeing a disturbing increase in is alternative "information" channels, ranging from news letters to satellite TV and computer whizbangery. These media supply zealots with only the facts they find it congenial to hear on whatever single topic obsesses them, from the purported constitutional right to bear arms to virulent hatred of abortion or homosexuals (or, typically, both). Hostility toward the mass media is rarely based on its pandering to egalitarian sluggishness. Rather, it is almost always based on what the press does well—conveying the facts about mainstream American opinion to people who want to believe that their hot corner alone represents the true nation.

For me the most unnerving aspect of the media decline is the tendency to treat science and reason as optional and to give a respectful place at the table to creationists, faith healers, herbalists and homeopaths, new age crystal worshippers, and other practitioners of magic and mumbo-jumbo. (It is amusing to contemplate the reaction of these assorted true believers to being equated and lumped together.) In an era when religion is the basis for shooting up a van full of teenagers or exploding the World Trade Center—not to mention what it leads to in Belfast or Bosnia—it might seem reasonable for journalists to approach religious fervor with some skepticism, or at least to maintain the traditional posture that it is something private and not to be asserted in public life. Instead, the CBS TV affiliate in New York City marked a "sweeps" month in February 1994 with a heavily hyped series on miracle cures, replete with assertions that prayer made the difference. Even when such stories are balanced, science and common sense are treated at best as just another point of view, with religious self-delusion taking center stage. Where, for contrast, were the anecdotes about regular churchgoers who kept praying and stayed paralyzed or died of cancer anyway? The CBS network gave prime time in 1993 to a "documentary" produced by an outside firm and not subjected to the network's news standards; it purported to provide scientific evidence for the existence of Noah's Ark. When a debunker who infiltrated the "research" process demonstrated that most of the testing was inadequate, suspect, or just plain fraudulent, no major news media jumped on the story, save for *Time*, in a crisp story by my colleague Leon Jaroff. The sins in this case were far worse than NBC's with the exploding truck, and the consequences in terms of public opinion were far more extensive. General Motors was no longer selling the truck. Christian churches are selling the Noah's Ark myth, and reaping donations, every day of the year. But the exploding truck story was one that everyone could comprehend and wanted to hear, while the refutation of the Noah's Ark story was trickier to tell and certain to bring retribution from the Christian devout. An elitist editor who believed his role was to teach would have run that debunking story even so. But most editors are egalitarians these days. As the president of one newspaper chain remarked to me: "The first thing our editors have to learn is that they are in effect the marketing directors of their newspapers. That is their primary role."

Tribalism and hypersensitivity are as conspicuous in the mass media as they are on campuses, and the result is the same: a deadening of rhetoric and a suppression of information. Two small examples, instructively typical precisely in that they occasioned little or no brouhaha, make this point. For the 1993 baseball All-Star Game, the shoe manufacturer Nike prepared a commercial set in the Dominican Republic, the homeland of a number of distinguished major league shortstops—or, rather, "La Tierra de Mediocampistas," as the thirty-second spot dubbed that island nation. In keeping with reality there, all dialogue and the entire voice-over script were in Spanish, with English subtitles. One might have expected this tribute to delight the Hispanic community. But Tony Bonilla, chairman of the National Hispanic Leadership Conference, based in Corpus Christi, grumbled in disapproval. The commercial's blemish in his eyes: its supposed implication that Hispanics do not want to learn English and assimilate. Said Bonilla: "A large percentage of the Hispanic population might find it insulting." Bonilla conceded that most Hispanics continue to speak Spanish and maintain their culture, and that while a majority speak English at some level of competence, a sizable minority do not manage even that. But a sweet and innocuous commercial merited his complaint, he said in effect, if its cultural celebration reminded anyone of politically awkward facts. The upshot was that the commercial disappeared after its debut, presumably forever.

Another example of hypersensitivity went altogether un-remarked upon, so far as I know, by anyone except the erst-while *Boston Globe* colleague who sent it to me. It was an obituary for a black ex-convict, aged forty, who died of AIDS acquired "from using drugs intravenously"—the words pre-sumably appended so that his family could tell the world he was not gay. The piece reported three times in a headline and six paragraphs that he had earned a high school diploma while in prison. It described plans for scattering his ashes in the Caribbean. It spoke of his hope of "salvaging his life upon his release." But it nowhere mentioned what crime had resulted in his going to prison.

In the scholarly realm, most thinking about culture these days is an attempt to redefine who makes the rules, or even to challenge the process of rule-making. As Terry Eagleton writes in TLS, "The point is not to scrape place as a poor cousin at the high-cultural table but to establish your proper autonomy." The principal device is by casting doubt on all absolutes, all assumptions, all heritage that is inconvenient to one's cause. Adds Eagleton: "There is no supposedly absolute value which is not vulnerable to a relativizing critique." This attitude is conspicuous in the revisionist line on ancient Greek culture, epitomized by a *New York Times* review in March 1993. Surveying a Metropolitan Museum of Art exhibition of classical sculptures which were on a rare tour from their homeland, *Times* reviewer Holland Cotter indignantly as-serted the primacy of contemporary theorists over the works themselves. "The world-renowned objects have been gathered not in the interest of new scholarship nor in an attempt to see with fresh eyes the complex society that produced them," Cotter complained, "but as a kind of travel brochure, replete with a jingoistic promotional title meant to perpetuate clichés about art and its meaning that recent art history has been trying to dislodge." Now, there's a frank confession of priorities, rooted in a sublime assurance that the opinions and values of one's confreres of today are surely superior to, and directly applicable to, the culture of the past—even though one would not for a moment consider that the superiority and applicability might run the other way. Cotter continued: "Classicism is not perfection in any absolute sense; it is a politically pointed concept that lends approval to one set of forms and ideas and excludes another set as imperfect, inferior, even dangerous. . . . For this viewer, the biggest problem with this show is . . . its refusal even to acknowledge the validity of the esthetic myths this show promotes, myths that lie at the very heart of Western culture. . . . One is advised to keep in mind the questions this show never asks and as a result can't begin to answer, for in a real sense they are what this exhibition is about." The "myths" and "questions" are never explicitly articulated anywhere in the review. The political assumptions that drive Cotter are never opened to debate. But the most striking notion is the assumption that two decades of obscurantist art history, rather than two thousand years of continuous contemplative appreciation of a particular ideal of beauty, is what the exhibition is "about" and is what should matter to its viewers.

I don't know Cotter even well enough to know if he is a he or she is a she, but I assume from such writing that he or she would share in the prevalent diminution of value of great artworks, particularly classical works, by defining them as part of the heritage of the modern-day nations that occupy the same terrain where the art was created long ago. When Melina Mercouri, former cultural minister of Greece, died in March 1994, it was widely noted that she had failed in her life's foremost undertaking, to win back from Britain the so-called Elgin marbles. These sculptures once adorned the Parthenon and were rescued by Lord Elgin during a period of

Turkish hegemony in Athens, when the ancient temple was used as a powder magazine. A few months before Mercouri died unfulfilled, the Russian government conceded having stolen from Germany during World War II the "Schliemann treasure" of gold from Hissarlik, Turkey, the asserted site of ancient Troy. Some scholars argued that Athens has a better case for repatriation of the marbles than Turkey does for repatriation of the gold, on the basis of a clearer line of cultural continuity between ancient and modern times. This attempted distinction was dismissed as "cultural elitism" in a *New York Times* letter to the editor by Patty Gerstenblith, identified as an associate professor of law at De Paul University in Chicago.

To me, this whole archaeological and anthropological exercise misses the point entirely. When works of art are of paramount beauty and importance, when they attain the status of universal significance—as is surely true of both these collections—they become the cultural heritage of the whole world. As their impact transcends national boundaries, any question of their ownership transcends mere geography. The Elgin marbles should stay in London, not by right of conservatorship or conquest, but because they will be seen by more people there. The same applies to restoring the Schliemann gold to Germany, after the Russians hid it from world view for half a century so as not to have to admit their thievery. These objects belong to the heritage of the planet. They should be placed wherever they are most apt to be visited.

The opposite posture to Cotter's relativizing of classic certitude is the supreme self-confidence in personally embodying the ideal. This stance is taken by such cultural traditionalists as James B. Twitchell, author of *Carnival Culture: The Trashing of Taste in America,* who argues, "We live in an age distinct from all other ages that have been called 'vulgar' because we are so vulgarized that we have even lost the word in common use, and, in a sense, the esthetic category." Paul Fussell says much the same in *BAD: Or, the Dumbing of America,* where he speaks of "the great crappiness that is essentially American." Interestingly, what binds together the extremes of relativism and certainty are a shared anger at the world as presently constituted and a shared sense of powerlessness to change it. In both cases what seems to be missing is the positive side of egalitarianism, the will to tolerance, coupled with the positive side of elitism, the intellectual suppleness to tolerate and accept diverse elements in society while holding firmly to one's own values.

Perhaps the best small but telling index of how relativist and intellectually insecure cultural thinkers are these days is the "unrequired reading" list drawn up by professors at the University of Buffalo in an attempt to seduce their students—college students, mind you, supposedly in the period of peak intellectual curiosity—into the simple act of reading for pleasure. On this list of "good but not necessarily great books," according to the undergraduate dean who headed the project, one will find no Shakespeare or Plato, although *The Adventures of Huckleberry Finn* did make the cut, side by side with such fiction as Ray Bradbury's *Fahrenheit 451,* Ralph Ellison's *Invisible Man,* Joseph Heller's *Catch-22,* and Katherine Dunn's *Geek Love.* The nonfiction list includes Daniel Boorstin's *The Discoverers,* Barbara Tuchman's *The Guns of August,* Dee Brown's *Bury My Heart at Wounded Knee,* and Ambrose Bierce's *The Devil's Dictionary.* A history professor chose *The Joy of Cooking* because, he said, it was a "how-to manual that is clear, explains the vocabulary and introduces students to the many cultures that inform our society."

Simple, useful, and politically correct. How much more could one ask of a work of literature? Well, a lot really. But not in these egalitarian times.

EIGHT

Politics by Saxophone

"We believe the promise of America is equal opportunity, not equal outcomes."
—Item in the 1990 declaration of principles of the Democratic Leadership Conference, William Jefferson Clinton, chairman

WHEN BILL CLINTON looks at himself in the mirror every morning, does he see a survivor who got ahead by elitist principles of hard work, study, classical scholarship, and general merit? Or does he see a lucky everyman whose rise is the result of the whims of fate? His family background is the stuff of liberal sob stories about those who never had a square chance. His roving father seems to have left illegitimate children scattered across the landscape. His multiply-married mother was a sometime victim of wife beating. His boozy stepfather set a pattern of substance abuse to which Clinton's drug-taking younger brother also succumbed. The household income afforded blue-collar privation, short of outright poverty but not always by much. The rest of the clan are no-accounts, and no-accounts they will likely remain.

But something propelled Clinton to the top, handshaking his way through high school and Georgetown and Oxford and Yale Law, shrewdly glomming on to people who would grow up to be noteworthy in their own right long before their status as Friends of Bill put them in charge of helping run the country. Surely the something that pushed Clinton ahead was more than accident, more than a nervous tic of natural charm. Surely he felt something of the same urgent need, and the same confidence in an orderly and meritocratic world, that impelled Harry Truman and Richard Nixon and Lyndon Johnson and Jimmy Carter to grow beyond humble origins. Clinton may presume to speak for the common man, but he knows he is an uncommon man. He is, as Nicholas Lemann suggested in a November 1992 *New York Times* op-ed piece labeled "The Smart Club Comes to the White House," a living symbol of meritocracy. Not only did Clinton make his career that way, he found his wife and almost all his friends through the system of education and achievement.

It is tempting to think that a man whose life and work were so defined by personal initiative will therefore shift the focus of national debate to reemphasize the individual and to diminish the expectation that government exists to overturn the results of competition and the marketplace. If Clinton's dropping of Lani Guinier as his nominee to run the Justice Department's civil rights office meant anything more than a politician's instinctual run for cover, it may have been a certification that he truly believes what he endorsed as chairman of the Democratic Leadership Conference in the document quoted at the beginning of this chapter.

But the process by which he got elected, the constituent elements of the Democratic party that carry out his directives in Congress, the media-dominated means of contemporary governance, and the lies and self-deceptions by which the electorate lives all militate against Clinton's expressing such views even if he has them. The ability of a man from Clinton's background to rise, in the systematic way that he has, ought to be the best possible testimony about what's right with America. Instead, it is all too readily transmuted into a symbol of unfairness, of the wickedness of elitism. His entree to his trio of illustrious alma maters is redefined as privilege rather than achievement. Unless he struggles to win the populist label himself, Clinton can readily become a victim of Perot-style populist rhetoricians and their politics of envy.

The most basic fact of life in presidential politics, an axiom of the current campaign trade, is the primacy of television. That is true in the most obvious sense. All campaigns are now constructed primarily to manipulate imagery on a large scale, through both paid and "free" media (the pols' quaint term for journalism). But in a larger sense the axiom mistakes the medium for the message. The most basic fact of political life,

driven by the rise of television and the consequent erosion of
the party structures, is that each member of the public now
feels entitled to a one-on-one relationship with a campaigner
and perhaps with a sitting president. People boast of "voting
for the man and not for the party" as though this were an
indication of moral and intellectual superiority, as though
they were transcending ideology rather than failing to engage
it. The relevant fact is not what a politician says or does, but
how likable he seems, how much trust and affection he in-
spires. This is almost equally true if one is appearing on television to hawk a book, anchor the news, or play pitch meister
for an automobile. People are reluctant to give you anything
they don't have to, even their time, unless they conclude you
are nice.

In the case of politics, the exchange is complicated by a
further degree of egalitarianism. Television has helped redefine representative democracy in a much more personal way.
A politician does not simply represent you in the sense of
holding the seat allocated to your place of residency or even in
the deeper sense of being expected to fight for your interests.
In the television era, a politician represents you—or is expected to—in the direct sense of sharing your worldview and
value system and therefore being a dependable alter ego, making decisions the way you would yourself if you had the time
and were in power. The fit is never perfect, of course; no one
can be all things to everyone, and the larger and more diverse
the constituency he represents, the more a politician is
tempted to blur his own views or to give contradictory signals
to fit each contrasting circumstance.

Part of this process is a distasteful egalitarian effort to present oneself as a "regular guy" when by definition anyone who
secures the presidential nomination of a major political party
belongs to some sort of elite. Usually it is an elite of high
office-holding and consequent power; frequently there is an
ancillary elite connected with the politician's education; more

often than not there is a further elite of birth or wealth or both. To achieve the aura of plainness, George Bush put out word that he loved pork rinds and country music (he didn't particularly fancy either of them) and he hoped that driving a high-powered motorboat, instead of taking a leisurely sail, would diminish the patina of privilege conferred by his world-class summer hideaway at Walker's Point in Kennebunkport. For Bill Clinton, whose own polls indicated that voters thought he had grown up rich because he had attended such plummy schools, the chosen symbols were junk-food gluttony and the saxophone. In an era when elitism was not so despised and was indeed to a degree expected of the Leader of the Free World, to appear on the Arsenio Hall show for a jam session would have been a gaffe of irredeemable proportions. When Harry Truman played the piano, after all, he did so at the White House—which is to say, his home. Clinton seemed like a rowdy out on a party night. I'm enough of a fuddy-duddy that I thought the saxophone caper might prove a fatal mistake even in our egalitarian times. In retrospect, it looks like one of the smartest things Clinton did in a very smart campaign.

The problem with fostering a personal link with the elec-torate is that this kind of pseudo-chumminess makes it diffi-cult to lead and inspire. It is not enough to be elected. A President must renew his mandate, in a close equivalent to campaigning, virtually every day—the ultimate triumph of populist egalitarianism. Americans who want to like their offi-cials and who think of them as down-home, folksy, just-like-me regular fellas quite naturally find it jarring when the leaders start to preach. Oh, a sermon about individual respon-sibility and self-reliance can start off well enough. Most of the population thinks of itself as much more hardworking and independent than it in fact is. The hard part comes when a leader starts to talk about specifics.

The trickiest matters for a President to discuss realistically with the voters have to do with payments unwisely dubbed "entitlements." In congressional parlance, this term means simply that such payments are statutory obligations of the government, at least in the absence of any corrective legislation. To the recipients, however, the word *entitlement* has a broader and more emotional meaning. This is money to which they are *entitled,* if not by virtue of mere citizenship, then as a by-product of a contractual relationship with the government. Thus these sums are, in their minds, immune from government scrutiny or reconsideration during shifts in policy.

This attitude applies to such absurdly costly items as military pensions, which by definition are paid to people out of whom the country is no longer getting any service, but who are more often than not employed and building up some other kind of pension credit. Other military benefits, including education and health care, are almost always wildly out of proportion to the salary and length of service, at least by the standards of the private sector. But then, people in the armed services theoretically put their very lives at risk (although millions of well-compensated veterans never faced anything more life-threatening than a chow line). There is therefore some basis for saying the recipients earned these benefits in the elitist mode of hard work—although the compensation often has the egalitarian intention of lifting the lower classes, from whom military employees most often come, into middle-class comfort.

Other entitlement programs involve an even greater measure of egalitarian wealth-sharing, accompanied by a far more intense elitist delusion that one is merely reclaiming what one already put in. Consider, for example, the Social Security program, the biggest of the vital lies by which the electorate lives. In an earlier chapter, Social Security was characterized as a welfare program. Mathematically this is undeniable. Every recipient who lives a normal lifespan gets back much more than he paid, even including a market rate of return. (The proper comparison for this calculation is passbook savings interest, which is similarly risk-free, although some advocates of the giveaway to the elderly seek to substitute the long-term growth rate of the stock market so as to make the overpayment look less extreme.) A median recipient recoups his contributions and "interest" in three to four years and then goes on to collect for another twelve to fifteen, after which a surviving spouse may collect for many years more. Low-income workers pay less and get less, but their percentage rate of return is even more generous. Despite the rhetoric of politicians over the years, there is no Social Security trust fund; the program operates on a pay-as-you-go basis, and it has an unfunded future liability that would get a corporate pension fund in big trouble with the law. As former United States Commissioner of Social Security Dorcas Hardy has written, "Social Security has always been a wealth transfer from young to old."

Recipients, willfully blind to the fact that they are taking a handout from the next generation, refuse to see the truth. "We paid our taxes, right the way along" is their (irrelevant) refrain. They cannot come to terms with the fact that their eligibility to receive a check has nothing to do with the *amount* of that check, which is legislatively determined. This stubborn incomprehension is not limited to the financially dim-witted. I have known retired business executives who went into frothing hysteria when anyone attempted to engage them in a pragmatic, rational discussion of the justice in their being so overpaid by workers of today.

It is no secret to anyone in official Washington that some presidential administration will have to address the skewed accounting of the Social Security system. Each President comes into office praying that it will not be his own. Ronald Reagan was the exception to this rule, and he lasted about a week in the trenches. After he proposed pushing back the retirement age, with the plan to take effect many years in the future, and was met with a virtual uprising, he did a complete volte-face. Soon after, when the number crunchers calculated that inflation was so low that Social Security recipients were not entitled to a cost-of-living increase one year, Reagan gave it to them anyway, further impressing upon the mass mind the idea that such increases were a contractual part of their "entitlement." Clinton has made no move to address the issue at all, save for the indirect means of trying to reorganize the health care system; health benefits are the fastest-growing cost item in the Social Security system. Everyone fears a political panic if national leaders acknowledge the truth, to wit, that the middle-aged and young will have to bear a great deal more responsibility for their retirement than the currently retired generation is doing. If those currently paying in to Social Security realize that it is in essence a Ponzi scheme, the thinking runs, they will seek to reduce the amount paid to the elderly or at least impose a means test on the recipients, which the elderly in turn will avenge at the ballot box. So the people still young enough to make sensible arrangements are left in silence when they need to hear the elitist message of self-help, while well-off elderly recipients who could do without all or some of their Social Security payments are spared the message that might shame them, or prick their consciences, into doing so.

Government leaders are even more quiet about a social and financial problem that is more immediate than the Social Security crisis and that probably dwarfs it in scope: what to do with the underclass. Four or five decades ago, union leaders and the occasional left-of-center philosopher fretted aloud about "automation" and wondered what the work force would do without work. That day has arrived and the answer is troubling. Where I get my check, and the same is probably true almost everywhere else, hundreds of employees have seen the tasks they used to perform taken over by computers or other mechanical devices. Meanwhile, the nature of the economy has shifted so that unskilled jobs pay less and there are many fewer of them. Although the American economy has a remarkable record of job development, there are more than enough displaced workers, women reentering the job market, and, yes, immigrants to absorb the new vacancies. Companies don't run large-scale training programs to help the underclass because, by and large, they don't have to. Inner-city schools are ineffective enough, and the teaching of values at home is hit or miss enough, that millions of young people emerge upon the world essentially hopeless. Whatever the future fluctuations of the economy, there is unlikely ever to be a place for them. Nothing will be done about the problem until it is acknowledged in the starkest possible terms—and in truth it is hard to think what could be done about the problem in any case. Our egalitarian myth is foundering on the rock of elitist reality. There are large numbers of Americans for whom America has no meaningful place.

This problem is not simply a matter of race, although some would have us think it so. In an August 1993 issue of *Newsweek*, general editor Michele Ingrassia could be read to have dismissed as "white values" the injunctions "Go to school, get a job, get married and the family will be just fine." She suggested that the growth of the drug culture came "as the legitimate marketplace cast [black men] aside. . . . The biggest culprit is an economy that has locked them out of the mainstream through a pattern of bias and a history of glass ceilings." In truth, from 1980 to 1988 the size of the black middle class grew by a third, from 3.6 million people to 4.8 million. Employment and family income grew at a much faster rate for blacks during that period than they did for whites. The problem is one of class—and of values. It is, of course, harder to make a good life if one comes from a dreadful one. But some people do make the leap to productivity. How are we to explain their existence, except by accepting the elitist dictum that some values and indeed some people are better than others, and should be encouraged?

Many people on both sides of the ideological divide speculate that the problems of the underclass could be alleviated by cutting down immigration, which during the 1980s accounted for about forty percent of the population growth and about twenty-five percent of new entrants into the labor force, according to George J. Borjas of the National Bureau of Economic Research, writing in an October 1993 edition of *Fortune.* The theory is that immigrants are, if not always limited to low-wage and low-skill jobs, nonetheless apt to take them—and to work cheap. During the 1980s, Borjas says, the share of unskilled immigrants among the high school dropout portion of the work force doubled, from one in eight to one in four. During that same period the wages of native-born high school dropouts fell ever further behind the wages of native-born workers with more schooling. In short, he argues, competition from immigrants drove down the bargaining power of the native-born. Borjas takes a more wide-ranging negative view of immigration, suggesting that immigrants receive federal Aid to Families with Dependent Children at a rate disproportionate to their contributions in taxes. On an annual basis, he says, the six hundred thousand or so legal immigrants increase national income by about four billion dollars—a gain, but, he adds, a "small" one.

An intangible or at least hard-to-measure factor that Borjas omits is the long-term, multigenerational contribution that immigrants make. In contrast to the native-born underclass, who tend to remain mired in a cycle of poverty, immigrants are generally upwardly mobile, generation by generation. They send their children to college and the children do well, then go on to improve on their parents' lot. Although Asians do especially well, the phenomenon cuts across racial lines. And it is most intensely observed among young people who are immigrants themselves. In contrast to the native-born, or even the American-born children of immigrants, children who are foreign-born tend to exhibit better work habits, get better grades, and otherwise exhibit traditional "Protestant work ethic" values far more than most actual Protestants. The longer they stay in the United States, however, the more the foreign-born tend to lapse into the laxity of their peers, according to Ruben G. Rumbaut, professor of sociology at Michigan State University and author of a study on the subject released at the annual meeting of the American Association for the Advancement of Science in February 1994. "The longer you are in the United States," he said, "the more you learn, among other things, the bad habits, such as wearing headphones while studying or waiting to the last minute to study for a test." Rumbaut analyzed school records of five thousand children in Miami and San Diego and found that those here for five to ten years had a grade-point average of 2.58 on a scale of 4.0, a bit ahead of American-born children of immigrants, whose average was 2.44. Other studies have established that children of immigrants, wherever born, outperform the American-born children of American-born parents. Rumbaut found that Vietnamese-born children, who typically had suffered the worst ordeal in getting to the United States, worked the hardest at school and did the best. Children born in Mexico did the worst, perhaps because their families had made the least unequivocal commitments to being truly American, or perhaps, Rumbaut suggested, because of poverty, discrimination, and low educational levels among their parents.

That explanation, common among liberal victimologists, may be facile, however. As Francis Fukuyama, author of *The End of History and the Last Man,* argues in an April 1993 essay in *The New Republic:*

Being a poor and persecuted outsider can also be a source of strength, because it forces the immigrant into a ruthless self-examination, reinforcing the values that are crucial for survival. One could argue for the importance of immigrant status by pointing to, among other things, the fact that immigrant blacks from the West Indies and other places tend to do much better as a group than American blacks descended from slaves. Older and more secure groups such as WASPS in America face decline precisely because their established social status deprives them of any need to claw their way to the top. By this line of reasoning, the great advantage of the lands of new settlement such as the United States, Canada, Australia and the like is that they are constantly being renewed in their social character by successive waves of immigration. . . . Their success, it can be argued, was due not just to their liberation from traditional culture, but to their acceptance of an old, uncorrupted Anglo-Saxon one in its place; it was a culture that promoted a kind of individualism that was open to constant innovation and change, but it also—and this aspect is too frequently underestimated—fostered a strong sense of responsibility toward family, community, and workplace that prevented the individualism from degenerating into anarchy.

Whether immigration is good or bad, the prospects for shutting it off are not great. The total number of immigrants in the U.S. is 19.8 million, according to Rumbaut, an all-time high. While some immigrants would be happy to shut the door now that they have come through, others have a sentimental attachment to opportunity or a pragmatic desire to bring in relatives, and they are too large a group to be ignored in a pluralistic political system. Besides, the nation's borders are porous. The subset of would-be immigrants who are apprehended coming in illegally, a fraction of those who try, amounts to 1.8 million per year. Realistically, we cannot close our borders. Veteran diplomat George Kennan argues in his 1993 musings *Around the Cragged Hill: A Personal and Political Philosophy:* "There are already far too many of us in the United States." But the pressure of would-be immigrants, he adds, will nonetheless end only "when the levels of population and poverty are equal to those" of the third world. The difference between the inescapable immigrants and the native-born underclass is the amount of effort each is willing to expend in attempting to escape that poverty.

The problems of the American underclass will not be made any easier by egalitarian outcry from the rest of the impoverished world. In an alarmist essay for the September 1993 issue of *Harper's,* Richard J. Barnet of the Institute for Policy Studies in Washington argues:

Across the planet, the shrinking of opportunities to work for decent pay is a crisis yet to be faced. The problem is starkly simple: an astonishingly large and increasing number of human beings are not needed or wanted to make the goods or to provide the services that the paying customers of the world can afford. Since most people in the world depend on having a job just to eat, the unemployed, the unemployable, the underemployed, and the "subemployed"—a term used to describe those who work part-time but need to work full-time, or who earn wages that are too low to support a minimum standard of living—have neither the money nor the state of mind to keep the global mass consumption system humming. Their ranks are growing so fast that the worldwide job crisis threatens not only global economic growth but the capitalist system itself.

Without needing to take so glum a view, one must admit the persuasive power of his statistics—not least about the United States, where, he points out, the Fortune 500 companies laid off some 4.4 million employees between 1979 and 1992, but also about such places as Mexico, Kenya, and Pakistan, where the labor force is growing by three percent per year while the economies are not. Barnet quotes Secretary of Labor Robert Reich as having observed that Japan has succeeded by an emphasis on "bringing the bottom half of its primary and secondary school population up to a minimum level of competence," in marked contrast to the absence of policy for elevating our underclass, or for that matter our population of ninety million illiterate or marginally literate adults. To embark upon such a policy would, of course, shatter the egalitarian myth that we are all more or less equal and all more or less good enough. It would require that Bill Clinton, an elitist success himself, acknowledge the deep gap between the accomplished and the barely functional and the bridge of skills acquisition that is the only way to cross that chasm.

The other fundamental issue on which a little more candor is in order is income distribution. There are three major rationales for a graduated income tax: to raise revenue for running the government, a purpose essentially everyone accepts; to acquire the funds from those best able to pay; and to redistribute incomes in the name of fairness—although it often looks akin to punishment for being well-to-do. Democrats have delighted not merely in taxing the affluent, but in baiting them and satisfying the petit bourgeoisie by suggesting that the gains of the rich are somehow ill-gotten. Many Democrats of my acquaintance share my feeling that it is one thing to be asked to pay taxes and quite another to be battered with rhetoric suggesting that one is really paying some form of restitution. In denouncing the Reagan years as an era of "reverse Robin Hood," Democrats have often brandished statistics based on after-tax income distribution rather than gross earnings, as though a tax cut amounted to a pay raise—or, rather, as though all of one's salary belonged to the government in the first place, and it was only Uncle Sam's beneficence that determines how much one should get to keep. This kind of talk reinforces the lottery mentality of the general populace, the view that success in life is not earned but happened upon by chance. Often it is accompanied by rhetoric suggesting that steep taxes on the rich would somehow eliminate the burden on everyone else, an assertion that is true only if one defines rich so broadly that it includes practically everyone below retirement age who owns his own house. As Kennan observes

Politics by Saxophone 209

in *Around the Cragged Hill,* "I know of no assumption that has been more widely and totally disproved by actual experience than the assumption that if a few people could be prevented from living well, everyone else would live better." The Democrats have an effective elitist message to offer in raising taxes —to wit, noblesse oblige—and most of the well heeled would respond enthusiastically to such a call if it were accompanied by leadership pushing the underclass and the working masses to take a more elitist line too—to ask more about what they could do for themselves and less about what government could do for them.

To expect such leadership of Clinton is to assume that when he looks in the mirror each morning, he sees himself as his own effort has made him and has the courage to say so in public. There is, alas, little reason to expect it of the man who boogied with Arsenio. As Sidney Blumenthal observed of a Democratic leader a decade ago in a shrewd *New Republic* essay, Ronald Reagan was Miller time and Walter Mondale the factory whistle. Clinton has no stomach for becoming the factory whistle, however much America needs to buckle down to work. It was as a Miller-time guy that he got elected.

The missing element in every phase of American life, from education to culture to the thicket of identity politics, is what used to be called rugged individualism. This sort of frontier self-reliance is utterly out of fashion. Environmentalists think that individual freedom threatens the ecoscape. Imposers of quotas and speech codes think that individualism threatens the civil peace and the process of defining and installing an up-to-the-moment definition of justice. Educators think that individualism liberates the strong at the expense of the weak. Politicians think that rampant self-reliance leaves too many people behind.

All of those are dangers, of course. Yet they are dangers that can be managed and are better not overmanaged. As British constitutional scholar Ferdinand Mount observed in surveying recent essays on the dangers of market-oriented democracy: "That is what politicians in liberal democracies are paid for, to ensure that rules are framed and administered so as to produce results which accord, so far as humanly possible, with our sense of justice and charity. . . . But like most things in life, the co-operative impulse has limits."

The emphasis on the dangers of individualism has obscured the virtues it offers, from the creation of jobs to the creating of art, from the awakening of ambition to the taking of risks to the imagination of new ways and new forms. Taking our identities from groups stimulates us to be like others, and therefore by definition not to be creative. Looking for equality of outcomes rather than equality of opportunity means relinquishing responsibility and control. Obsessing about justice and fairness too readily leads to succoring the disadvantaged instead of urging them to make the best of their circumstances. Individualism maximizes human potential and ultimately propels the whole human race forward, albeit admittedly at different rates of progress. The expectation that our leaders will represent us literally, that they will be nice guys in the same way that we fancy ourselves to be, deprives us of leadership that can inspire and challenge and demand, and replaces it instead with leadership that simply smooths out the bumps of a static life. Egalitarianism is supported most strongly, of course, by the half of the population that is below average and that therefore gets a better deal out of egalitarianism than it ever would out of elitism. But the lower half could not prevail without the moral surrender of much of the upper half, which generates most of the wealth that society has available to divide.

This surrender has been engendered mainly by doubt—doubt about the moral value of the American past, doubt about the legitimacy of American dreams and ideals, doubt about the right of those now advantaged to lay claim to the fruits of their labors, doubt about the very merit of competition. The emergence of these doubts is in some way a credit to the refined sensibilities of contemporary Americans. But great nations are not built on doubts, and in the chaotic world of the present, America is needed as a model of greatness.

We cannot, of course, put the genie back into the bottle. Serene confidence about everything in the American experiment, from the civilizing value of Columbus's voyages to the conquest of the plains and mountains to the rough-and-tumble process of assimilation in the melting pot, has given way to an edgy relativism that insists on viewing things from all sides without embracing any of them. The historic and in some cases present grievances of women and blacks and Hispanics and Asians and gays and so many others are real, and the urge toward recompense among the alleged oppressors is reinforced by righteous indignation from the downtrodden.

But we can draw comfort from a few undeniable facts. The rest of the world wants to come here because America is better—not just economically better but politically better, intellectually better, culturally better. Ours is a superior culture, and it is so precisely because of its individualism. More than any other world power, in fact, we gave to global consciousness the very idea of the individual as the focal point of social relations—not the king, not the army, not the church, and not the tribe. Just when the world is rushing toward us and our ways, let us not slide toward embracing theirs.

The past that made our culture is a seamless web. The attitudes one may lament in the present are inextricable from the attitudes that spawned a desirable modern world. And the past need not be ashamed of itself, nor we for it, that it included racism and sexism and homophobia and other offenses against modern notions of human rights. Human beings are an evolving species, morally as well as biologically. To get to where we are, we had to come from somewhere less humane. An imperfect world is not the same thing as a worthless one.

Accepting that people have varying gifts and abilities and will arrive at varying outcomes is not diminishing their humanity. Rather, it is more demeaning to engage in the egalitarian deceit of equating achievements and outright charity.

Above all, fairness is not the same thing as equality. It is unfair to the able to deny them special programs for the gifted, to impinge on their attainments, to take a larger share of their money away in taxes simply to deprive them rather than to raise revenue. It is unfair to men and whites and children of privilege to hold their achievements suspect. It is unfair to women and blacks and the poor to create compensatory programs so pervasive that they can never know with full confidence the joy of having achieved something entirely on their own. A fair society is one in which some people fail— and they may fail in something other than precise, demographically representative proportions.

It is hard to take so dispassionate a view when so many people seem frustrated, even in pain. The Bill Clinton who urged equality of opportunity rather than of outcomes is also the Bill Clinton whose health care plan envisions shunting medical students primarily toward family practice and tightly limiting access to the specialties—and then earmarking places in each of them for racial and ethnic minority groups!

This is not hypocrisy on Clinton's part, or at least it is not *just* hypocrisy. We have become accustomed to identifying unequal outcomes as a problem, to looking to government to solve the problem and to imposing cumbersome regulatory mechanisms to mediate against the harshness of fate. Both elitism and egalitarianism have a place in the American debate.

But in the battle between them, in every corner of our intellectual and political life, the wrong side has been winning. To speak in defense of elitism is not to tilt the balance of national life, but to seek to restore it.